Leaving Scotland

Mona McLeod

NATIONAL MUSEUMS OF SCOTLAND

Published by the National Museums of Scotland
Chambers Street, Edinburgh EH1 1JF

ISBN 0 948636 83 1

© Mona McLeod and Trustees of the National Museums of Scotland 1996

British Library Cataloguing in Publication Data

A catalogue record for this book is available from the
British Library

Series editor Iseabail Macleod

Designed and produced by the Publications Office of
the National Museums of Scotland

Printed on Huntsman Velvet 110gsm by
Clifford Press Ltd, Coventry, Great Britain

Acknowledgements

We are grateful to the National Museums of Scotland Charitable Trust for
support for this publication.

Illustrations: Front cover: Glasgow Museums and Art Galleries. Back cover:
Glenbow Museum, Calgary. 4, ii bottom, 42: Hugh Cheape. 7, 9, 11, 16,
26, 39, iii, xii, xiii, xiv, 45, 51, 73: National Museums of Scotland. 17:
Inverkeithing District Library. 23: Royal Castle, Warsaw. 24, 29, 57, 63:
Trustees of the National Library of Scotland. 28, i bottom, 48: Mona
McLeod. 32: Colonial Williamsburg Foundation. 33: Muscarelle Museum
of Art. 36: Edinburgh City Art Centre. 37: Eastern National Park and Mon-
ument Association. i, 71: Scottish Record Office. ii top: King's College,
Aberdeen. iv top: Queen Victoria Museum, Launceston. iv bottom:
Tweeddale District Museum Service. v top: David Livingstone Centre. vi
top: National Library of Australia. vi bottom: Kirkcaldy Museum and Art
Gallery. 49: National Army Museum. 53: Sheila Brock. 59: Mrs J C
Somerville. 68: Otago Settlers Museum. 70: by permission of the Syndics
of Cambridge University Library. 78: Andrew Carnegie Birthplace,
Museum.

Front cover: *Detail from* The Last of the Clan. Tom Faed, 1865

Back cover: *John Rae, Arctic explorer, in the dress of a Cree
Indian.* William Armstrong, 1862

CONTENTS

INTRODUCTION

For hundreds of years Scots have been leaving home. In the twelfth century David I had to invite foreigners to Scotland to people the new burghs he was founding, but by the fourteenth century the tide had turned. Scottish migrants had become a European phenomenon and a Frenchman could write:

Mark you what the proverb says
    Of Scotsmen, rats and lice
The whole world over, take your ways
    You'll find them still I guess.

Why did our ancestors emigrate? Where did they go? What happened to them?

Poverty has always been the main reason for leaving Scotland. Two thirds of the land is harsh – rocky, ill drained, swept by rain-bearing winds off the Atlantic and far from the Mediterranean and the medieval centres of European trade and culture. But the westerlies which brought the rain could also blow the enterprising Scot to the mainland of Europe. Of the hundreds of men who left home few came back.

The medieval travellers found themselves on a continent where Latin was a common language and the church knew no frontiers. As missionaries, pilgrims, crusaders and students they set out for great shrines of Christendom such as Jerusalem, Rome, and Compostela. Scholars like Duns Scotus studied and taught in the European universities; crusaders such as Douglas, who set out to carry Bruce's heart to the Holy Land, never came

An advertisement of 1872 in English and Gaelic, promoting emigration to Canada by steamship.

back. Scottish Christians were part of a European community into which they could be easily absorbed, but probably most ended their days in Scotland.

Soldiers were much less likely to survive, or come home. When not fighting the English, thousands of Scots became mercenaries, employed first by the French and later by the Dutch and the Swedes. Officers sometimes came back with foreign wives and titles, but more died fighting beside their men. Their reputation became formidable and, after the Union of 1707, Scottish regiments served the British Empire in every part of the world. The Scottish soldier fought, bred and died abroad.

It was the traders who founded the first Scottish communities away from home. By the thirteenth century they were settling on the Baltic coasts, taking out cargoes of salmon and hides and bringing back timber and furs. A century later a Scottish staple – a port through which all exports had to pass – had been established in the Netherlands, first at Bruges and later at Vere. Wool from the Border abbeys and salt from the Forth were being exchanged for fine cloth and Rhine wines. Burgesses from the royal burghs were sending out their sons to study the techniques of European trade. Many intermarried and settled abroad. Scottish gates, Scottish quays and Scottish streets began to appear on the maps of Europe.

Adventurers, social misfits, political and religious refugees had been leaving for hundreds of years, but in the seventeenth century a new factor was driving Scots away from their homes. Schools in Lowland parishes were producing a literate population: five universities in a country of under a million people created a highly educated middle-class. In an underdeveloped economy there were few middle class jobs. The great brain drain started. Most took the high road to England and became English, but those who emigrated to the economically backward Baltic states remained stubbornly Scottish. Poland had become 'The Heaven of the nobility, the Paradise for the Jews, the Hell for the peasant, and the gold mine for the stranger.' In Protestant Sweden the strangers were easily assimilated, but in Orthodox

Russia or Roman Catholic Poland they remained separate communities, inter-marrying and keeping up their contacts with Scotland. Right up to the twentieth century they were making substantial contributions to the economic development of their adopted countries.

For many Scots, however, leaving home has meant the British Empire. Long before the Clearances, emigrants from the Highlands had been taking a Gaelic culture to North America. True emigrants, they knew they would never return and created communities which, for several generations, remained distinctively Scottish. Glasgow merchants trading in tobacco with Virginia or

The Hudson's Bay Company supply ship Prince of Wales. *The Company recruited many Scots to crew their ships and as traders and trappers. Detail from a watercolour by Robert Hood.*

sugar with the West Indies seldom settled abroad, and the East India Company servant, if he survived long enough, always brought his fortune home. Walter Scott was to describe India as 'the corn chest for Scotland'.

The nineteenth century opened up new opportunities. In Africa Scots went as missionaries, explorers and traders; less often as farmers. Land and labour required more capital than most would-be emigrants to South Africa possessed. In the Far East traders were forcing open the ports of China and Japan and missionaries followed. But for the impoverished Scot Australia and New Zealand were the lands of opportunity. Free land and an assisted passage, hard work and much suffering could lead to independence if not affluence.

The British Empire, in which the Scots played so important a part, no longer exists, but economic pressures are still driving Scots from Scotland. Wherever they go they are likely to find themselves in the footsteps of their fellow countrymen and, like them, will leave their mark upon the world.

LEAVING SCOTLAND

1 Medieval Europe

In twelfth-century Scotland there were probably fewer than half a million people, scattered more evenly over the country than they are now. Land over 1,000 feet was too cold and wet for cultivation and low ground was often marshy or covered with forest. Viking invasions had weakened links with the Mediterranean and cultural contacts were with Ireland rather than with mainland Europe. Towns, trade and industry scarcely existed. Scotland was economically underdeveloped. So the early Scottish burghs attracted foreign immigrants and David I's charters were addressed to his 'Scots, French, and Flemish burgesses'. In 1150 he sent 'Mainard, an experienced Flemish burgess of Berwick to help the Bishop of St Andrews to create a burgh round his

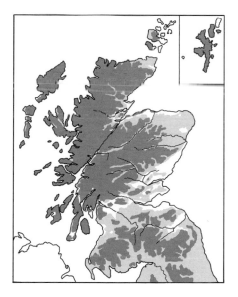

Map of Scotland. The shaded area shows land difficult or impossible to cultivate. Tim Smith

☐ *Best land*
▨ *Medium land*
■ *Harsh land*

cathedral and a few years later a Scandinavian called Knut was performing the same role at Roxburgh.

For another hundred years Scottish merchants stayed at home and incomers to the new burghs gradually became Scots. But clerics had always been part of an international Latin-speaking church. From the seventh century Celtic monks were bringing Christianity back to Europe where it had been destroyed by barbarian invaders of the Roman Empire. From Lindisfarne in Northumbria to St Gall in Switzerland the 'Scotti' of Ireland and Iona founded churches which were to become, in south Germany, the 'Schottenkloster'. By the fifteenth century the Irish monks were being replaced by Scots. At Ratisbon, Erfurt, Wurzburg, and Kelheim these Sottish communities survived until the nineteenth century. Scottish merchants who had been settling round the monasteries since the early Middle Ages were granted full citizenship of their adopted cities.

The Benedictine monks who came to Scotland in the eleventh and twelfth centuries would also have close contacts with the continent. Every year abbots were expected to visit the mother house and both abbots and bishops had to be confirmed in their office by the Pope. Appeals from clerical courts were heard in Rome and general councils of the church were held in southern Europe. In 1420 sixty Scots attended the Council of Basle, probably taking hundreds of junior clerics with them. Until the Reformation a constant stream of churchmen and their servants must have crossed the Alps.

Pilgrims set off on the same route. First a safe passage through England had to be secured. There they would visit the tomb of Thomas à Becket at Canterbury before starting the long pilgrimage through France, visiting shrine after shrine until they reached the final goal in France, Spain or Italy. The poor rarely got further than Whithorn or St Andrews, but for the rich, pilgrimages were great adventures. They stayed in the guesthouses of monasteries, the hospices of the Templars, or the castles of their peers. Macbeth reached Rome in the eleventh century when the English envoy commented sourly that 'He scattered largesse like seed corn to the poor.' In the fifteenth century the Earl of March was keeping open house in Paris. Pilgrims enjoying his hospitality were reported to be 'Well dressed and elegant ... well thought of for their spirit, virtue and generosity.' So much money was leaving Scotland with these wealthy pilgrims and their servants that Stewart kings were reluctant to grant 'passports to cross the sea to the Holy Land'.

The Holy Land was the goal of the Crusaders, but few reached it, many dying on the way. Although 'a battalion of brave Scots' had fought with the Earl of March and St Louis of France at Tripoli in 1287 most Crusaders were landowners. A few were lured by promises of castles and land, but for the majority a Crusade was the greatest of pilgrimages, ensuring forgiveness of sins and certain entry into Heaven. The Fairy Flag at Dunvegan is probably a trophy brought back by a MacLeod who survived the long and hazardous journey to the East.

Jet figure of St James, probably brought back from a pilgrimage to his shrine at Compostella in Spain, sixteenth century.

The Scots most likely to leave home for good were the scholars and students. Until the fifteenth century there were no universities in Scotland and even in the sixteenth George Buchanan, James VI's tutor and one of the most distinguished scholars in Europe, could call Scotland, perhaps unfairly, an intellectual desert. Before the Wars of Independence students had gone to Oxford or Cambridge but after 1296 they had to go further afield. There were Scots in all the great universities of Europe. Students lived in 'Nations'. In Paris there was a Scots College, but more often they were lumped with the 'Germans', along with Finns, Poles, Bohemians and Swiss. Life was hard. Students had to wear clerical dress, speak only Latin, and keep the peace. They were not, in theory, allowed to carry swords, dance, enjoy music, chess, dice, taverns, sport or go whoring. The laundress had to be 'old and ugly'. Many students were registered as poor. When 'utterly poor' they would be excused fees and the presents normally given to examiners before the exam and the traditional feast after it. James Douglas, the son of the murdered Black Douglas, was declared to be a pauper, but John Kennedy's claim to financial aid was challenged. He was found to be 'of noble blood, the nephew of a bishop, and the receiver of 150 crowns and 20 nobles'. His plea was dismissed.

Many graduates of foreign universities who came back to Scotland became leading clerics, lawyers and doctors. Great scholars were more likely to stay abroad. Duns Scotus, Adam of Gullane, John Major, Matthew of Scotland are just some of the names we know. After studying in St Andrews and Paris George Buchanan taught in France and Portugal before politics brought him back to Scotland. In a world in which Latin was the spoken language of the educated, they moved freely as teachers in the universities of Europe. Florence Wilson of Elgin is typical of others who remained abroad as schoolmasters. After graduating at Aberdeen he went to Paris to continue his studies in philosophy. There he became tutor to the nephew of Cardinal Wolsey and later master of the school at Avignon. The magistrates were so delighted that this Scot 'from the uttermost part of the earth' could teach Greek as well as Latin that they rewarded him with 100 gold crowns. Doctors who trained abroad, usually at Salerno in Sicily, often stayed abroad. Thomas Urquhart of Cromartie found a Dr Leath practising in Paris in the seventeenth century. 'As in the practice and theory of medicine he excelled all the doctors of France so, in testimony of the approbation he had for all his exquisiteness in that faculty, he left behind him the greatest estate of any of that profession then, as the vast means possessed by his sons and daughters there as yet can testify.' The successful stayed on and were absorbed into the country of their adoption.

Long before the sixteenth century merchants were doing the same thing. Although most goods entering Scottish ports were carried in ships of the Hanseatic League, monks from Melrose were exporting wool to their warehouses at Boston in Lincolnshire. In the Netherlands Scottish merchants were selling it to the cloth manufacturers of Flanders. Fine cloth and other luxuries came back, but many of the merchants remained in communities where, as at Campvere, they had their own church and enjoyed special privileges. In the Baltic, trading in salt and timber, they settled in ports like Danzig and Lübeck. And through these ports the poorest of Scots, the packmen, were begining to make their appearance. Lumped on their arrival with Jews and vagabonds, many were to become part of a merchant aristocracy. By the end of the Middle Ages, as clerics or laymen, the Scots who settled abroad could have been counted in their thousands; thousands more crossed the North Sea as soldiers.

2 The Scottish soldier

The Scots had established their reputation as mercenary soldiers by the early Middle Ages. The fourteenth-century chronicler, John of Fordun, quoted Isidore of Spain 'The Scots are quick and fiery of spirit, fierce to their enemies, loving death itself as much as slavery ... They are a people of sparing diet, bearing hunger long and rarely eating before sunset ... And though they are fair of face and of comely bearing they are much disfigured by their dress.' A hard country produces hard fighters: medieval Europe provided a market for them.

By the twelfth century England and France were the most powerful kingdoms in Europe. Under her Angevin kings, England was well governed and rich, an expanding and imperialist power. The Capet kings of France were overlords of an even richer country but had little real control over their ambitious vassals. Amongst these were the kings of England. They paid homage for Normandy, Brittany, Anjou, Maine and Aquitaine; in the fourteenth century they claimed the throne; in the fifteenth Henry VI was crowned king of France. Conflict was inevitable and, herself threatened by English imperialism, Scotland became a major recruiting ground for mercenaries. With a flourishing economy France could afford to employ them and Scotland's backward economy, like Switzerland's, ensured a supply of men. The Auld Alliance, which linked Scotland with France against their common enemy, provided the necessary political framework.

Recruiting followed a familiar pattern. Licensed by the king, ambitious vassals, a Douglas or a Buchan, raised companies from the adventurous, the unemployed and the feckless. Shipped out on foreign boats and paid by foreign monarchs, they fought and died abroad. There were no free passages home and neither pay nor booty to be won during the winter months. Thousands died in the French wars and after the Battle of Verneuil a mass was said for the souls of the dead by John Carmichael, the Scottish bishop of Orléans. In 1419 three hundred of the survivors became the Scots Guards, the bodyguard to French kings till the eighteenth century. But most of the common soldiers were left to forage for themselves and France became a prey to marauding bands. Those who did survive and settle were granted common citizenship after the Battle of Baugé, where 12,000 Scottish troops had helped to reverse the English victory of Agincourt.

Officers often fared better than the men. Sully, Colbert and Molière all claimed descent from Scots who stayed on in France and some, like the Earl of Darnley, were ennobled. Charles VII's citation of 1422 read 'At our prayer and request he came out of Scotland and brought with him a great company of men at arms and archers to put into effect the ancient alliance of the Kingdoms of France and Scotland ... the flower of the enemy is dead or taken ... that his service be for ever remembered he and his descendants may bear for ever in their arms the escutcheon of France.' Darnley was killed a few years later fighting with the French at Orléans.

Recruiting was mainly in the Lowlands; Highlanders in the medieval period were much more likely to serve as mercenaries in

Ireland then in France. As heavy infantry or gallowglasses they did much to defend Gaelic Ireland against the Anglo-Norman invasion which set up a state based on Dublin. When James VI succeeded to the English and Irish thrones in 1603 that military market closed, but the Reformation had opened up others. It changed the political scene and split Europe into two camps. When Spain attacked Protestantism and selfgovernment in the Seventeen Provinces of the Netherlands their Estates turned to Scotland for help. Textiles and trade produced the wealth needed to pay mercenaries and Scotland could provide the men. The Scots Brigade, founded in 1579, was not disbanded till 1781. Though most of the men were by then Dutch, a hereditary cast of Scottish officers was still giving the commands in Scots. The Brigade had made an important contribution to the victory of the Northern Provinces. James VI and I, trying to pacify the Borders, encouraged recruiting. He was only too pleased to see Kerrs, Hepburns and Armstrongs fighting abroad. Survivors were easily assimilated by marriage into the tolerant and international communities of the Dutch Republic.

By the seventeenth century the Counter Reformation had engulfed Europe in war, and Danes, Poles and Swedes were competing for soldiers. Like the Dutch, the Swedes were short of men rather than money, and in Gustavus Adolphus – 'The Lion of the North' – they had a commander whom any mercenary would be glad to serve. He cared for his troops and led them to victory. During the Thirty Years War there were probably 8,000 Scots fighting at any one time and the officers had command over English and other foreign troops as well as their own. Gustavus complained bitterly to James VI when some, under a Robert Stewart, changed sides and fought for the Catholic Poles. 'These are men of your nation (of whom many have fixed their business and homes amongst us) held in the highest honour in these kingdoms, and many are in command in our army, all enjoying as much as though they had really been born here, the rights and privileges of nobility.' Fortunes could be made, widows were

Scottish soldiers at Stettin in 1631. Over 20,000 fought for the Protestant cause under Gustavus Adolphus of Sweden during the Thirty Years War.

given pensions and a second generation was absorbed into the growing middle class. But the common soldier was more likely to move to another field of battle, with its opportunities for pay and pillage, than to settle in a community where his dislike for hard work was as well known as his love of fighting.

Russia attracted the officer class. Serfdom provided unlimited manpower but there was almost no middle class from which to draw leaders. Tam Dalyell commanded armies against the Tartars and returned in the 1660s 'a Muscovy beast who has roasted men'. General Patrick Gordon helped to create Peter the Great's army in the late seventeenth century and Admiral Samuel Greig Catherine the Great's navy in the eighteenth. Count Otto Douglas became governor of Finland and Prince Barclay de Tolly, whose family were originally Barclays of Towie, was a marshal in the army that fought Napoleon. But there was no mass recruiting of men.

After the Union of 1707 the role of the Scottish soldier changed. No longer a mercenary fighting for others, he played a vital part in the creation of the British Empire. The first kilted regiment – the Black Watch – was formed in 1741-2. It mutinied when ordered abroad, but abroad was where Highland regiments went. After the failure of the Jacobites in 1746, chiefs whose lands had been forfeited for rebellion became eager to earn Hanoverian favour by recruiting amongst their former clansmen. But after 1756, when 10,000 Scots fought in the Seven Years War against France, they were still mistrusted by the English. To quote General Wolf, 'They are hardy, intrepid, accustomed to rough country and no great loss if they fall. How can you better employ a secret enemy than by making his end conducive to the common good?' Those who survived the appalling conditions and harsh discipline were offered free land at the end of the war 50 acres for a private, 3,000 for a captain. They brought out their families and many became Americans.

Admiral Samuel Greig left Inverkeithing to become one of Russia's 'most accomplished and devoted naval commanders'.
Ivan Argunov

In the nineteenth century the Empire spread in all the continents; the map became red. Scottish soldiers left home to serve in every part of the world, often in hostile climates but as part of a professional standing British Army. They left behind them a formidable reputation and the association of the Scot with tartan and pipes. Few soldiers settled in India, fewer still in Africa, more in the Antipodes. It was the civilians working in temperate climates who were most likely to create Scottish communities overseas.

3 Merchant adventurers

The Mediterranean and the North Sea were the two major exchange zones in medieval Europe. France, Scotland's ally, lay between north Italy and the Netherlands, the two wealthiest urbanized regions. By the thirteenth century Scots merchants had established colonies in France, in the Netherlands at the mouth of the Rhine and at Baltic ports. But they had few ships and, till late in the fifteenth century, carrying trade was dominated by the Hanseatic League. These German merchants had privileges in Scottish ports which were not reciprocal and Scottish pirates had a more formidable reputation than had her traders. Ships' captains venturing to Bordeaux for wine or salt were as likely to be attacked by their own countrymen as by the English. It was the sixteenth century before Scotland had a merchant fleet and substantial numbers of her merchants were settling abroad.

Scotland's main exports were wool, hides and salmon and the Netherlands were her chief market. The cloth industry of Flanders needed the fine wool produced by the farms of the Border abbeys and through Bruges or Antwerp Scotland could import luxuries manufactured in the Netherlands, the Mediterranean or the Far East. The privilege of trading abroad was limited to the royal burghs and it was the burgesses and their sons who founded the first significant communities abroad. At Bruges, Middelburg and finally Vere the Scottish staple was established, with its own privileges of self-government and a church which, after the Reformation, sent representatives to the Assembly in Edinburgh. Political and religious refugees in the seventeenth century were often supported by a large and wealthy community of Scots, and Grand Tourists like James Boswell were entertained by relatives who had married into the Dutch aristocracy and could act as their bankers. The Hopes became the biggest bankers in Amsterdam and never forgot their Scots origins. However, it was in the Baltic countries that Scots found almost unlimited opportunities.

By the fifteenth century the Hanseatic merchants were losing their monopoly of the carrying trade of northern Europe but could still prevent settlement in German towns. It was through the free port of Danzig that Scottish adventurers entered Poland. In a country of serfs, governed by an increasingly powerless king elected by an over-powerful aristocracy, there was virtually no middle class. Lowland Scots of all social classes poured in, welcomed by monarchs who were looking for colonists for Lithuania, recently united to Poland by marriage, and a merchant class to supply their needs.

In 1598 the English traveller Fynes Morrison could report that 'Scots flock in great numbers into Poland

The Scotch house at Vere, the Scottish staple in the Netherlands.

rather for the poverty of their own kingdom than for any great traffic they exercised there, dealing rather for small fardels than for great quantities of rich wares.' They might start as peddlers or *kramers*, sharing the status of 'Jews and other vagabonds', but some became *Mercatores Aulici*, merchants under the special protection of the king, acting as bankers and suppliers of luxuries to an extravagant court. Whenever possible they sent home to Scotland for 'Birth Brieves' to prove their gentle birth. Some of their ennobled descendants were still living in Poland in the twentieth century. At the other end of the scale, in the late sixteenth century, were 'the great number of boys incapable of service and destitute of means of living ... yearly transported to the East Seas ... and there many times miserably dying and giving scandal'. James VI prohibited 'All masters of ships to transport any youths ... but such as shall be sent for by their families dwelling there or such as shall carry with them sufficient means of support for at least one year.'

Poland had become 'The America of the day' and by the seventeenth century over 30,000 Scots were believed to be living there. Brotherhoods of 'honest Scotchmen trafficking in Poland, Prussia, Germany etc.' were ordered by James to welcome and register newcomers, provide churches, schools, hospital beds and insurance schemes. 'An abundance of gallant rich merchants' traded in fish, coal and coarse cloth and sent back cargoes of flax, hemp and corn. Charles II, an impoverished exile in Holland in the 1650s, tried with minimal success to tax them. Andrew Dixon complained that, as a merchant resident in Cracow for over 37 years, he did not feel responsible for the financial difficulties of the King of Scotland. Many identified with Poland, Ferguson the banker building the first presbyterian church in Warsaw and a Cockburn the first commercial academy in Danzig. Others like Robert Gordon, whose fortune founded the College in Aberdeen, maintained their links with home. But for all of them Poland had indeed become 'the goldmine for the stranger'.

Sweden, Protestant and with a flourishing economy, provided opportunities for the enterprising. Trade was in copper, iron, timber and munitions. Merchants from Leith or Montrose often became industrialists and within a generation were being absorbed into Swedish society – 'All the best trade they draw to themselves' complained the Swedes. Half the burgesses of Stockholm were reported to be of Scots origin by the mid-century and 36 families had been ennobled.

Discharged soldiers were encouraged, as potential taxpayers, to settle in towns and in the eighteenth century they were joined by political refugees. Some were like the Jacobite John Mackenzie, heir to the forfeited Cromartie estates. He served with distinction in the army but returned to Scotland, with a Swedish title, to recover his estates. Another Jacobite was Thomas Erskine. Born in 1746, the year his family estate of Cambo in Fife was forfeited, he emigrated at the age of thirteen and started his career in the office of George Carnegie in Gothenberg. Within a few years he was a partner in another shipping firm and by 1794 had his own company trading in iron, timber, tea and oriental luxuries with Scotland, Canton, India and the USA. In 1769, when to play billiards in public premises was illegal, he founded the Bachelors' Club 'for billiards and pleasant undisturbed fellowship'. Most of the Scots who were amongst its founder members stayed on but, by the end of the century, Erskine had been able to buy back Cambo House and, inheriting the title of Earl of Kelly, returned to Scotland.

There was no equivalent to the Scottish Brotherhoods of Catholic Poland. The farmers, blacksmiths and mechanics sent out by Kelly to help his landowning friends to modernize their farming merged as easily into Swedish society as the merchants, doctors and financiers. Colquohun would become Cahun, Macdougall Duwall and Maclean Makeleer.

4 The brain drain

Since the early Middle Ages there has been a brain drain from Scotland. Duns Scotus, one of her most distinguished fourteenth-century scholars, taught in France and Germany and it was in Cologne, not St Andrews, that students gathered round him and a university was founded. Her scholars were teaching philosophy in Geneva, civil law in Augsburg, astronomy in Munich and inventing a form of shorthand in Leipzig long before there were universities in Scotland. By the seventeenth century the trickle became a flood. The Calvinist insistence on Bible reading produced a high level of literacy, and grammar schools fed into universities where fees were low. The search for employment drove many graduates abroad. For those born after 1603 the high road led to England but for many the Scots communities around the Baltic promised a warmer welcome. Latin was still the language of educated people and for gifted scientists, doctors and teachers there were few closed frontiers.

Some were born adventurers, such as one of the Aberdeen-shire Gordons. Leaving home in 1651 he wrote 'My patrimony being but small, the younger son of the younger brother of the younger house, I resolved to go to some foreign country, not caring much on what pretence or to what country I should go.' But as a Catholic he had little choice. He was educated at the Scottish seminary in Ratisbon and had to find work abroad. Robert Erskine, the sixth son of Sir Charles Erskine of Alva, did better. One of 30 surgeons recruited by Peter the Great, he had studied in Edinburgh, Paris, Utrecht and London and was a Fellow of the Royal Society. In 1705 he became Court Physician and a Councillor of State. On a salary of £700 a year he was able to send money home to his mother and endowments for hospitals and orphanages in Scotland.

Doctors were paticularly successful. Dr Henry Blackwood, a contemporary of Mary, Queen of Scots, was Dean of the Medical School in Paris, and Peter Lowe, whose *Whole Course of Chirurgie* was published in 1597, became Physician to Henry IV of France. Jacob Robertson of Struan was doctor to both Gustavus Adolphus and Queen Christina of Sweden, while John Johnston, who had studied at St Andrews, Leyden, Frankfurt and Heidelberg, became Royal Physician and Professor of Medicine at Warsaw in 1631. One of the most remarkable was a Blackwell, son of the Provost of Marischal College, Aberdeen. He graduated at Edinburgh in 1722 but 'urged by ambition and restlessness to see the world and seek his fortunes elsewhere' he became a printer in London, studied medicine in Leyden and Aberdeen and published an *Illustrated Herbal* and *A new method of improving wet and clayey ground*. He was invited to become Physician to the King of Sweden and Director of the Royal Farm. His mistake was to enter politics. Accused of plotting against the King, he was tortured and killed.

By the mid-eighteenth century Scottish education was being transformed. New schools, the academies, were teaching modern languages, navigation and surveying as well as the classics, and scholars who had studied in the Netherlands brought back the latest scientific approach to their universities. Natural philosophy and mathematics had always been taught alongside rhetoric, moral philosophy and theology in university curricula. Now chemistry began to develop. The Enlightenment was producing another generation of highly qualified graduates for whom there were too few jobs at home. Emigration was often the only alternative to a poverty-stricken life as a village schoolmaster.

And so they swarmed across Europe. They served congregations like the one at Königsberg which used the hall of the Castle until money from Scotland helped them to build their own church. The first sixteen pews, marked with the lion rampant, were reserved for Scots and a school and a burial aisle were added to the church. It was the nineteenth century before communities of this sort merged with the German Protestants living in Poland.

Banking was another field in which Scots excelled. Successful merchants became moneylenders: by the seventeenth century they were international financiers. Piotr FergusonTepper, grandson of a Scottish immigrant, was banker to the last king of Poland, a Maclean of Duart was advising the Queen of Sweden, a Rutherford and a Sutherland were bankers to Peter the Great and John Law was Controller General of Finance in France. To

Otto Ferguson-Tepper in 1785. His father was banker to the last king of Poland and a descendant of Alexander Ferguson who left Scotland in the early seventeenth century, became a merchant and founded the family's fortune. F A Lohrmann

quote R W Harris 'He had a clearer idea than most people of his day of the commercial revolution which was taking place in western Europe.' His grasp of the need to expand credit to secure economic growth led first to a boom and then to a slump which destroyed his career. Descendants of the more conservative Hopes of Hopetoun are still bankers in the Netherlands.

The contribution made by academics was probably most highly valued in Russia. Less than three per cent of her population lived in towns, illiteracy was widespread and her need for foreign experts was urgent. Henry Farquharson went from Marischal College to found the Moscow School of Mathematics and Navigation in 1701 and employed several Scots professors.

The Edinburgh Evening Courant *advertisement which brought 140 Scots to St Petersburg to work for Charles Cameron, one of Catherine the Great's favourite architects.*

For her Majesty the Empress of all the Ruffias.

WANTED,

TWO CLERKS, who have been employed by an Architect or very confiderable Builder, who can draw well, fuch as figures and ornaments for rooms, &c. &c.

Two Mafter Mafons,
Two Mafter Bricklayers,
A Mafter Smith, who can make locks, hinges, &c.
Several Journeymen Plafterers,
Several Journeymen Bricklayers.

It is expected that none will apply who are not fully mafters of the above work, and who cannot bring with them proper certificates of their abilities and good behaviour.

The mafter mafons, bricklayers, and fmith, muft have been employed as forefmen in their different lines. The mafter bricklayers and men will have a pice of ground given them. As the encouragement to each will be confiderable, the beft of tradefmen will he expected.

For further particulars apply to Meffrs Peter and Francis Forrefter and Company, Leith, who will have a good veffel ready to carry them out by the 1ft of April next, provided the Baltic is by that time open.

John Robinson returned from the Naval College at St Petersburg to take up the chair of natural philosophy at Edinburgh. There he taught mathematics, mechanics, hydrodynamics, astronomy, optics, electricity and magnetism; men of this calibre often came back. Another Edinburgh graduate, Dr Guthrie, wrote the first *Dissertation on the Antiquities of Russia* and Charles Cameron, invited to St Petersburg by Catherine the Great, brought out over 60 Scottish tradesmen and their families to build palaces, hospitals, bridges and barracks.

The attractions were real – passage out, a good salary, free accommodation and guaranteed employment. James Watt refused to go to Russia but an Adam Smith took out Scottish engineers and workmen to set up a steam pumping system for the dry dock at Kronstadt. Gascoigne, the bankrupt inventor of the rapid-firing canon called the carronade, was lured out by a salary of £2,000. Many of these families stayed and their sons, educated in Scotland or Germany, contributed to the development of Russia in the nineteenth century.

5 Industrialists and farmers

In the 1670s Charles II's Privy Council received a request from Jamaica 'that all prudential means be used to encourage the Scots to come hither ... and to prevent them going to Poland and other foreign nations'. Scots did in their thousands emigrate to the Americas: why in the nineteenth century were they still going to Poland and Russia?

Perhaps the answer lies in the trade figures for the east coast ports. The Baltic countries still provided wheat, rye, flax, iron and timber while a rapidly industrializing Scotland exported manufactured goods and salt fish. Her merchants were familiar with the underdeveloped economies of the Russian Empire and were ready to seize the opportunities they offered. If a venture failed the journey home was a matter of a few days: back from America could take three months.

Portrait of Adam Smith by John Kay. Some of the Polish landowners who attended Smith's lectures offered incentives to Scots to emigrate and introduce new farming methods to their feudal estates.

David Hume believed that Poland was the most backward state in Europe but under her last king, Stanislas Poniatowski, the Enlightenment reached Warsaw. Foreigners flocked to a brilliant court and Polish aristocrats on their Grand Tour discovered Edinburgh. Landowners and their sons sat at the feet of Adam Smith, visited Scottish farms and factories and returned determined to transform their estates. The Partitions, which placed Poland under the rule of Russians, Austrians or Prussians, robbed them of their political role and made the economic one ever more important. Their estates were vast, they could command capital and cheap labour and they discovered that skilled Scots could increase dramatically the productivity of land previously farmed by serfs. By the 1820s over 300 'English' gardens had been created, often by Scottish gardeners. Inspired by enthusiasm for Walter Scott, mansion houses were being rebuilt on the model of Abbotsford. General Pac went further and persuaded at least 80 families to come out to his Lithuanian estates. Recruited from Lowland farms hit by the depression which devastated agriculture after the Napoleonic Wars, they founded tightly knit and inter-marrying communities. New Scotland, Berwik, Govenlock and Linton appeared on the estate maps and Scotch carts, cheese, and swing ploughs, turnips, potatoes and crop rotations were introduced.

The Hays, Dicksons, Stuarts and Broomfields, lured by special privileges and low rents, brought East Lothian farming methods with them. Incomes trebled. Contemporaries were amazed. 'They are altogether of thrifty habits ... in the fields they are more hardworking than the local peasants ... although they pursue the most common tasks about the farm everyone of them knows how to write and calculate and some of them have collections of different kinds of books and they sometimes read them.' Many became gentleman farmers and estate owners. Some of their sons entered the Polish professional classes; others returned to Scotland for higher education and never came back. The failures were likely to be packed off to some distant corner of the British Empire.

Another group were the industrialists. In 1805 Count Zamoyski set up the first agricultural machinery factory using machines smuggled out from Britain and artisans lured by high wages and assisted passages. Krystyn Szmyrna, later professor of philosophy in Warsaw, came to Scotland in 1823 as tutor to Prince Czartoryski. They attended classes at Edinburgh University together and Szmyrna spent four years in Scotland. He visited every factory he could, pleaded ignorance of engineering and made sketches of any machine he thought might be used in Poland. A few years earlier Count Potocki and Alexander Kedslie had been fellow students at Edinburgh University. When Kedslie's corn business was in financial difficulties in the 1820s the Count persuaded him to emigrate and introduce steam power to the mills on the Potocki estates. Some years later Kedslie was teaching Poles to drive steam engines on the newly opened railways.

The pattern was repeated throughout Poland. After the failure of the 1831 Rising 8,000 of its leaders fled to Paris and 180,000 of their followers were sent to Siberia. Having destroyed the intelligentsia, the Russian government had to recruit in western Europe for the engineers, industrialists and professionals they desperately needed. The Scots who responded, attracted by higher salaries than they could get in Britain, often contracted to pass on their skills to Polish apprentices and act as consultants. Three generations of Garvies, descendants of a Paisley-shawl weaver from Penicuik, became managing directors of a textile factory at Zyrardow which, by the 1890s, was employing over 9,000 people and producing the finest linen in Europe. Poland became the most industrialized part of the Empire.

Russia provided a vast market for Polish goods but the Russian social pattern was different. Until 1861 serfdom was firmly entrenched and the aristocracy excluded from productive occupations. Her tiny middle class was politically powerless and initiative had to come from the czars. Corruption and inefficiency reigned. But here again enterprising Scots found opportunities. A government delegation recruited workmen in Glasgow to build the railway from Moscow to St Petersburg. Started in 1837 with serf labour it had made little progress; the Scots completed it in four years. Steam engines from Stephenson's works in Northumberland were being replaced by the end of the century with ones from Richard Smith's boiler works in St Petersburg. After serving an apprenticeship with the Caledonian Railway he came out on a seven-year contract in 1847. He had his own works by 1856 and ran the firm with great success until war and the Revolution

The gold medal for linen was presented to Thomas Garvie at the Paris Exhibition in 1900.

Charles Baird's Ironworks in St Petersburg were based on experience gained at the Carron Works, where he was head of casting and ordinance before emigrating.

destroyed it in the twentieth century. Entrepreneurs, engineers and financiers working in Russia in the nineteenth century were often second- or third-generation Scots.

By the twentieth century they had contributed substantially to the modernization of western Russia. They became fluent in Russian, Polish, German and French and moved freely around the Empire. But they retained their presbyterian faith and British passports and kept out of politics. In 1914 those who could got out: those who remained were to see their work and their homes destroyed.

6 New Scotland? – the aborted empire

James VI's accession to the throne of England pacified the Border but created a new problem – the former reivers 'of whom the country is full for want of employment, now that the general peace has been restored between England and Scotland, and at the same time great distress has arisen from the excess of population'. Some went off to serve as mercenaries in Europe; others traversed the narrow strip of water, so often crossed by settlers, to move into Ulster. But in a predominantly agricultural economy problems remained. A series of cold springs and wet harvests could reduce subsistence farmers to starvation; fisheries were in the hands of the Dutch; without wider markets industry stagnated. Economic growth was extremely slow.

Raleigh had advocated the settlement of Virginia, and James too looked to America. The merchants who had financed the early ventures were determined to keep out competitors but, in Nova Scotia, James hoped to found a Scottish colony. Sir William Alexander, Earl of Stirling, poet, courtier and a remarkable man, became proprietor. His problem was how to people it: James's solution was to create baronets. For the payment of 1,000 merks and the settlement of six families, an aspiring Scot could get 10,000 acres and a hereditary title. He could take possession on the esplanade at the castle in Edinburgh and never cross the Atlantic. The land-hungry, who did, struggled for ten years to create farms out of forest, only to find themselves pawns in a diplomatic game when Charles I gave the territory to France. It was 1713, when Britain won back Nova Scotia from the French, before Scots were able to settle there again.

But English colonies were open to Scots in the seventeenth century either as proprietors or servants. Religious dissidents like Sir John Barclay of Urrie, a Quaker, was one of five Scottish proprietors in New Jersey. In South Carolina Sir George Campbell and Sir John Cochrane were granted land where the London government hoped that Scots, known to be tough fighters, would prove a useful frontier force. Within a few years, however, their settlement at Stuartston was destroyed by Spaniards and Indians.

As servants they were more welcome than as proprietors. Of these, hundreds reached America as prisoners. Those taken at Dunbar or Worcester during the Civil War were sold to planters and farmers. Freed after serving a seven-year sentence, they were forbidden to return. The Covenanters who survived shipwreck on the voyage to the West Indies were often used to supervise slaves on the sugar plantations of Barbados or Jamaica – 'the grave of the Scotsman'. They were joined by Jacobite prisoners in the eighteenth century, when a third of the white population of the Carribean was believed to be of Scottish origin.

Indentured servants came out voluntarily. In 1647 David Peebles bought 833 acres on the St James river. He ordained that 'by sound of drum' a proclamation should invite men and women to go out to 'create ane plantation there', and sixteen indentured servants went out to Virginia with him. But most, the adventurous or the desperate, bargained with a shipper in Aberdeen or Leith and were then sold to an employer in America. A legal contract could bind them for one to seven years to work for food and clothes and the promise of tools and land at the end of their service. The death rate was high. But in 1684 Peter Wilson, formerly a messenger in Selkirk, could write home to his cousin, 'Poor men like myself live better here than in Scotland, if they will but work.' After a four-year indenture he was farming 25-30 acres at 2d per acre rent and a share of the crop. The system was still working in New York State in 1805 – 'A wench – 8½ years of time of a healthy wench for sale. She is honest and sober and undertakes the work of a family generally.' In Boston in 1657 the first of many 'Charitable Societies' was set up by successful Scots to help these new immigrants.

Most Scots reached America by the back door; a few came in at the top. Presbyterians, excluded from high office by Charles II and James VII, were emigrating till 1688: after 1688 Episcopalians were filling pulpits in Virginia and one of them, Commissary

The College of William and Mary was founded in 1689 in Williamsburg, then the capital of Virginia, by the Scottish Episcopalian James Blair.

James Blair, founded the College of William and Mary one of the first universities in America. More bitterly resented by the English upper classes were the highly-educated Scots who were being appointed to important posts in the crown colonies. There were Scottish Governors in New York, Virginia and Pennsylvania and in New Jersey the Secretary, Attorney General and Clerk to the Supreme Court were all Scots. Challenged by their rivals in London, the judges found in their favour – 'A Scotchman born is by law capable of being appointed a governor of any of the Plantations, he being a natural born subject of England in Judgment and Construction of Law as much as if he had been born in England.' Direct trade with the colonies alone remained illegal.

In the 1690s, a decade of famine and dearth, Scotland made a last attempt to found a colony of her own. According to English but not Scots law Glasgow merchants trading with Newfoundland, Virginia and the West Indies were acting illegally. The Company of Scotland trading with Africa and the Indies was set up to break into a lucrative trading area but was diverted by London opposition to Central America. And so the Darien Scheme was launched. A Scottish colony on the Isthmus of Panama was to become a centre of world trade, an outlet for Scottish manufactures and a home for emigrant Scots. It proved a total disaster, ill planned from the start and deliberately sabotaged by William III. Of the 151,000 who set out in 1698 for the disease ridden Isthmus, half died. The 13,000 who followed them were attacked by the Spaniards who claimed Panama as their territory. Escaping to Jamaica, hundreds were drowned and the few survivors settled in the eastern colonies. Scotland was drained of men and money. Bitterly humiliated, their failure to found an empire was one of the factors driving Scots towards the Union of 1707.

The Rev James Blair arrived in Virginia in 1685. He was appointed Rector of Williamsburg, Commissary of the Province, President of the Council and, for 50 years, President of the College. John Hargreaves

7 After the Union – the British Empire

After the Union of Parliaments in 1707 Scottish traders could no longer be treated as smugglers and the demand for settlers and soldiers grew. Grants could be cancelled if land was not settled within a few years, so proprietors and their agents were competing for emigrants. Wars against France and Spain required soldiers in America and India as well as in Europe; administrators were needed throughout the Empire. Social and economic pressures in Scotland made it the ideal recruiting ground.

The Glasgow tobacco merchants were the first to benefit from the Union and families like the Hamiltons were typical. The father managed the Scottish end of the business while his son and nephew were in Virginia. There they bought tobacco, stored it in 'factories' by the James River and had it ready for loading as soon as boats docked. The cargoes brought out from the Clyde – iron ware, coarse cloth for the slaves and European luxuries for their masters – were sold in stores belonging to the company. Tobacco became the currency with which the planters paid their debts. The Hamiltons owned 'stores, warehouses, hatters, tailors, blacksmiths, coopers, taverns, plantations, wagons and river vessels'. Careful management at the American end made a rapid turn-round possible. 'Glasgow people have become almost the sole engrossers', complained a London merchant. 'The Scots sail their ships so much cheaper than you can from London and they have other advantages to which you and I are strangers ...' Amongst these was a tradition of university education at home and simple living in Virginia. Over 80% of tobacco imported was re-exported to continental Europe. From the east coast port of Montrose the Coutts, originally corn merchants, sent one son to Maryland and another to Virginia and traded with America, Scandinavia and the Baltic. Coutts' Bank was founded on the fortune they built up on this triangular trade.

In 1776, when war broke out between Britain and her American colonies, the Virginian planters owed £1,306,000 to the Clyde merchants. Unable to sell tobacco except through British merchants and encouraged to buy on credit from their stores, most ran up debts which sales of the season's tobacco crop failed to clear. Many of the merchants, like the Spiers, had seen the storm clouds gathering and had already moved into the West Indian sugar trade. A few were Patriots and remained. More were Loyalists who left Virginia to settle in the Carribean or to return to Scotland. When the war ended in 1783 some debts were repaid and some compensation made for confiscated property, but many hard-earned fortunes were lost.

In the eighteenth century individuals were still going out as indentured servants but increasingly Scots were emigrating as whole communities. The enclosure movement brought wealth to some but poverty to more. Peasant farmers had no security of tenure and rack renting could turn them into landless labourers. Rents went up by as much as 400% in the Lowlands, 300% in the Highlands. Thousands moved to the central belt, but emigration might seem preferable to ill-paid work, appalling conditions and periodic unemployment in the factories of the growing industrial towns. Thousands who did find work in a boom were driven out by dire poverty in a slump. So emigration societies flourished.

Friendly Societies would help an individual craftsman and his family to emigrate, and skilled workers would be welcomed in any newly-estabished community. By the mid-century farmers in Galloway, Stirlingshire, Ayrshire and Perthshire were organizing emigration on a large scale. Agents were sent out to the middle colonies to negotiate for land and the farmers followed. Less reputable agents were advertising in *The Gentleman's Magazine* in 1749:

Let's away to New Scotland where plenty sits Queen
O'er as happy a country as ever was seen
And blessed her subjects, both little and great
With each a good house and a pretty estate.
No land lords are there the poor tenant to tease
No lawyers to bully, no Bailiff to seize

The reality might be very different. The journey could take three months in conditions worse than those on a slaver and half of the passengers might die. Arriving too late to clear the land or sow a crop, the survivors often had to depend on the charity of earlier settlers to get through the first winter. A community of 300 who had followed their piper from Killin to the Clyde were piped ashore in Nova Scotia in 1776 to discover that their 'farmland' was uncleared forest. But the Scots had come from a hard country and many made good. Soldiers discharged after the French wars who took up their land grants were joined by their families. Letters home could paint a glowing picture of a land of

*'The Caledonian voyage to money-land', a contemporary
cartoon caricaturing the hopes of success in the New World.
'Gin I get to money-land I wanna come back,' says one.*

opportunity: whole communities responded. One dramatic
response was from the Highlands.

Long before the 1745 Rebellion or the Clearances, overpopula-
tion had been driving Highlanders south. The movement was
accelerated by the destruction of the clan system, which made both
the clansmen and the tacksmen, the officer class of the chief's
private army, redundant. Soaring rents and bad harvests might
drive them off the land and sheep farmers would move in. Allan
Macdonald of Kingsburgh, Flora Macdonald's husband, was
typical. He had lost nine-tenths of his cattle in the famine years
1771-74 and sold the rest to buy land in North Carolina and pay the
passages of his family and 60 of his clansmen. In 1773 James
Boswell reported from Skye – 'Mrs Mackinnon told me that last

year, when the ship sailed from Portree for America, the people on shore were almost distracted when they saw their relations go: they lay down on the ground and tore the grass with their teeth. This year there was not a tear shed. The people on shore seemed to think that they would soon follow.' Many of these tightly-knit Highland communities survived in the Carolinas and Nova Scotia. By the end of the century Lady Linton, the wife of the English ambassador, found that Gaelic was being spoken by black slaves and was still needed in the law courts. Amongst the 180,000 who crossed the Atlantic in the eighteenth century, language, dress and traditional clan loyalties often delayed assimilation into American society. But Scottish governors such as Gabriel Johnson did all they could to encourage settlement and London welcomed the fighting qualities of Scots on the frontiers of the Empire.

The Rev Dr John Witherspoon became Principal of the College of New Jersey at Princeton in 1768. He encouraged his fellow Scots to emigrate and was the only minister to sign the Declaration of Independence. Charles Wilson Peale

To the independence of America Scottish professionals made a significant contribution. A foundation had been laid by graduate teachers and ministers who had been lured out by free passages and excellent prospects. Leaving a country whose constituion made a mockery of democracy, they found themselves politically emancipated. Writing from Pennsylvania in the 1770s one minister reported 'With respect to our laws, they are made by those who are not nominally only, but really, our representatives for, without any bribes or pensions, they are chosen by ourselves and every freeholder has a vote.' The Rev John Witherspoon was first Principal of Princeton, and Edinburgh graduates founded

America's first medical schools. The philosophical pragmatism of the Enlightenment played an important role in the growth of the colonies to nationhood and second-generation Scots were often Republicans. Witherspoon, who was the only minister to sign the Declaration of Independence, was one of the authors of the Consitution. At the inauguration of Washington as first President of the Republic the Guard of Honour was commanded by General Malcolm, wearing the kilt. It was the newcomers who had emigrated in the 1760s and '70s who were more likely to remain loyal to George III.

When the American colonies became the USA in 1783 thousands of these Loyalists made the long trek north into Canada. Emigration to the States started again in the 1790s. The USA was always the main destination for nineteenth-century Scots emigrants. They provided their quota of presidents, governors and millionaires, entrepreneurs, black sheep and failures but they left home as individuals to become Americans. It was to the new British Empire that Scottish communities were to go.

8 Canada

The Loyalists who moved to Canada were to discover that to earn a living there was an even tougher proposition than it had been in the States. Scots had been trading in furs and fishing from Newfoundland ports since the seventeenth century and the Hudson Bay Company had been recruiting its best agents and trappers in the Orkneys – 'not turbulent Scottish fools but sturdy, inoffensive crofters and fishermen who needed no instruction about northern hardship'. But the Company wanted agents to deal with Indian hunters of the far north, not migrants. The Sinclairs of Caithness, who were principal shareholders, made sure that part of the men's pay went directly to their families in Scotland.

Alexander Mackenzie, a Stornoway man employed by the North West Fur Company, was one of many Scots who were to extend the frontiers of this northern empire. He explored the

Labrador coast in 1789, sighted Vancouver Island from the Pacific in 1792 and made the first crossing of the Great Divide. He was followed in the search for the North West Passage by Ross, Scoresby, Parry, Mackintosh and Maclean. The most remarkable of these men was Dr John Rae. An employee of the Hudson Bay Company, he walked the 5,300 mile northern coast line in eight months, trapping and fishing as he went. Although the explorers defined the frontiers of Canada they could do nothing to make settlement easier in a country of virgin forest, empty plains and Arctic winters.

When the States won their independence Lower Canada – Quebec – was already settled by French and English. The 30,000 Loyalists who sailed from North Carolina and the 81,000 who trekked from the Hudson valley settled in Nova Scotia and Upper Canada. There were thousands of Scots amongst them: thousands more were to cross the Atlantic in the next century. Pushing westward from the Great Lakes, they were the first settlers in six of the new provinces, effectively blocking the expansion of the

Scots employed by the Hudson's Bay Company collected
Canadian Indian material for the newly-founded Museum of
Science and Art in Edinburgh. These Chipewyan mittens were
collected by Bernard Ross in 1862.

USA. Why, from an apparently prosperous Scotland, were whole communities still making the appalling crossing to such an inhospitable land?

In the nineteenth century there were several new factors driving people from their homes. By 1820 industrialization had reduced the wages of handloom weavers from 25 shillings a week to five shillings, threatening the most skilled of craftsmen with beggary. A slump could lead to massive unemployment for the less skilled. When kelp as a source of potash was replaced by imported chemicals in the manufacture of soap, Highland landowners no longer needed a large work force for cutting and burning seaweed; this at a time when potatoes as a field crop and improved medicine were producing a population explosion.

Between 1800 and 1825 Glasgow's population grew from 70,000 to 170,000 and in the Hebrides the increase varied from 50% to 200%. With sheep farming still bringing in large rents and the railway making the Highlands accessible to southern sportsmen, crofters were in the way. Emigration – encouraged, assisted or enforced – seemed to many landowners the best way of reducing the population.

The Earl of Selkirk approached the problem as an idealist. He learnt Gaelic, engaged a doctor, and went out to Nova Scotia with the Highlanders to whom he lent tools, seeds and money. Three more settlements were planned in Upper Canada: all but one failed, defeated by climate, mosquitoes, wolves and, in 1812, renewed war with the USA. Few loans were repaid and Selkirk returned to Europe impoverished and disappointed. Another Gaelic-speaking community from Glengarry which followed its Catholic priest to Nova Scotia survived. But as late as 1838 Lord Durham could report: 'A very considerable part of the Province has neither roads, post offices, mills, schools nor churches ... and a widely scattered population, poor and apparantly un-enterprising though hardy and industrious ... living in mean houses, drawing little more than a rude subsistence from ill cultivated land.'

Patent of nobility granted by King Henry IV to David Kinloch in 1598 in recognition of his services to France.

The arms of the Douglas family with the Winged Heart, in memory of the 'Good Sir James' who set out in 1330 to carry the heart of Robert the Bruce to the Holy Sepulchre. Falling in battle against the Moors in Spain, he threw it towards Jerusalem, crying 'Forward Brave Heart'.

King's College, Aberdeen was
founded in 1495. Its graduates
often emigrated to find work.

Lübeck in the seventeenth
century. Scots had been settling
in Lübeck and other Baltic
ports since the thirteenth.

A caricaturist's impression of Highland soldiers who took part in the occupation of Paris after the defeat of Napoleon.

Tasmanian settlement sketched by naturalist Robert Neill, who left Scotland in 1820 at the age of 19. His first job was as a clerk in Hobart's Commissariat Department. G N Swinney

Mungo Park of Selkirk, the first European to set eyes on the River Niger in West Africa.

Thomas Baines, who painted this watercolour, was one of six assistants who accompanied David Livingstone on his travels up the Zambesi river.

St Andrews Church, Madras.

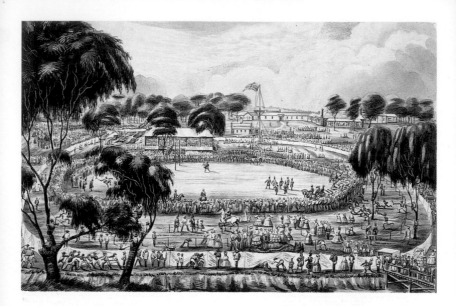

The first meeting in 1860 of the Bendigo Caledonian Society, established by the Scots who poured into the district during the gold rush of the 1850s.

John Macdouall Stuart who, in 1863, was the first white man to cross Australia from south to north.

Scots and their French allies fighting the Russians in the
Crimea, 1854

Personal belongings of John Rae, carried with him on his Arctic explorations.

Emblem of tobacco sellers. In the eighteenth century the tobacco trade with the American colonies contributed enormously to Glasgow's and Scotland's economic success.

In spite of hardship letters home drew people across the sea. John Gemmill could write to his son in Glasgow in 1827 'I am extremely grieved to hear of the distress that prevails in Scotland ... if any of our friends are labouring under the present calamity, I would advise such of them to embrace ... the opportunity of emigrating to this country ... for in the course of a few years hard labour they would find themselves independent of their fellow creatures.' Emigration societies proliferated. The Bridgate Transatlantic was typical. It had over 8,000 applicants from friendly socieies for aid to settle in Canada. Nearly 2,000 were helped to leave Scotland.

These were the voluntary emigrants. The Clearances drove whole communities off land on which they had no security of tenure. In order to make it more of a sporting estate Sir James Matheson, whose family's firm Jardine Matheson had made a fortune from the opium trade in China, cleared 21,000 tenants off Lewis. But he did provide transport, supplies and some financial aid for their journey to Canada. Gordon of Cluny, hoping to sell Barra to the government as a convict island, drove 1,500 people off his estate, whipping the more reluctant onto the boats. The experience of the Sutherland emigrants must have been typical.

The old and the children could not stand the hardship of the voyage, every day one or more of our group was buried at sea. After tossing on the Atlantic for eleven weeks we came to the coast of Canada. Each day we had to pay for our food and as some of us had some money left the Captain cruised up and down for three weeks before landing us penniless on the Canadian shore. We were taken by bullock wagon to Toronto. There we stayed in sheds put up for the emigrants. Small-pox was raging and carried off many who had survived the voyage. Then we were given an Indian guide, a sack of maize-meal, a sack of seed potatoes and a plough. We marched a hundred miles and were left in the middle of a forest to make our homes. We had to burn down the trees before we could plant the potatoes. For six months we had nothing to eat but maize-meal and water.

*Pages from a Gaelic pamphlet showing 'before' and `after'
illustrations of Manitoba, to encourage emigration from the
Highlands.*

The attitude of successive governments varied. Concerned by the loss of manpower and capital, the Passenger Act of 1802 was intended to check emigration by raising its price; the 1815 Bathurst settlement for discharged soldiers encouraged it. Fearing American expansion, 41,000 were to be settled on the frontier. Lured by a free passage and a grant of £15 per man and £2 for a wife, 100 acres of land and six months' supplies, 700 emigrated. The colony grew slowly. By the mid-century both the Canadian and British governments were financing emigration and by the 1880s steam-boats and railways were reducing the horrors of the journey out. Settlement on the prairies of Manitoba was marginally easier than in the forests of Ontario.

At a time when Gaelic was under attack in Scotland its value in isolating emigrants from the dangerously revolutionary ideas of the American republicans over the border was recognized by Selkirk. So a Celtic culture has survived to the present day, kept alive in churches, schools and newspapers and in Celtic societies wherever Highlanders have settled. Till the 1930s communities arriving from Scotland were welcomed and supported by third-generation Gaelic-speaking Canadians. 'Every Lewis man would get a job.'

There are over two million people in Canada of Scottish origins. What have they brought to their adopted country? In politics they worked for increasing self government and Dominion status. Lord Elgin, when governor, recognized the importance of a Canadian representative assembly. A Macdonald was the first Prime Minister and a Mackenzie the first Liberal one. Another Mackenzie was the first Mayor of Toronto. John Galt the novelist founded Guelph and his son Alexander was called 'the Father of the Constitution'. In engineering, finance and education they played an equally prominent role, creating the railways, canals, universities and colleges which are their lasting monuments. And the ordinary Scots brought a stubbornly independent spirit to the peopling of Canada.

9 India – the corn chest

In *The Men Who Ruled India* Philip Mason described the Scots as 'sons of the manse, younger sons of the big house, sons of doctors and crofters, more industrious than the English, less aloof, hard headed but emotional, more romantic at heart'. A century earlier Walter Scott had called India 'the corn chest for Scotland where we poor gentry must send our younger sons as we send our black cattle to the south'. What drew the Scottish upper classes to India?

Scott had half the answer. There was real wealth in Scotland but not enough to support a high standard of living for a large family. The East India Company, a fiercely protective company of London merchants, had been set up in 1602 to trade in the luxuries of the Orient. By the late eighteenth century it had become the virtual ruler of the states in which it had treaty ports. The great Moghul Empire was disintegrating and French and English were competing to control as many as they could of the princely states. The Company needed agents, administrators and soldiers: Scotland provided them.

There was no question of emigration. Climate, religion and culture were totally alien and the men who went out intended to come back. Until it was abolished in 1858 the East India Company had three regional armies, predominately Indian, but with European officers. Regular regiments of the British Army also served in India. Conditions were tough. There were no married quarters for the men and it was the nineteenth century before the wives of officers began to join them. Conditions on troop-ships were even worse than those on emigrant boats and many men died during the four-month journey out. The reputation of the Highland regiments was outstanding; fifteen men were awarded Victoria Crosses after the relief of Lucknow in 1858. But more died from disease and infected wounds than were killed in

Cover of sheet music for 'The advance of Sir Colin Campbell', hero of the siege of Lucknow.

THE ADVANCE OF SIR COLIN CAMPBELL.

WITH THE

BRAVEST OF THE BRAVE.

DESCRIPTIVE OF THE

FALL OF LUCKNOW.

ARRANGED FOR THE PIANO-FORTE

BY

JOHN PRIDHAM.

Pr. 2/6

battle. The death rate amongst the officers was equally high. Wars to drive the French out of south India were followed by wars of annexation to drive the Russians back from the North West Frontier. Scots commanded Indian troops as well as British and an hereditary caste of officers was created.

They left home tragically young. Twelve-year-old boys would be sent to England to train at Woolwich or the Indian college at Haileybury, where they learnt Persian, the official language of government and law till 1833. Sir James Malcolm, the son of an impoverished landowner, had command of two companies of soldiers by the time he was fourteen. A brilliant linguist, he was sent on a mission to Persia and in 1815 published a two-volume history of the country. He ended his career as governor of Bombay with a salary which would be the equivalent of millions now. Amongst many distinguished generals who were knighted were Hector Monro, Governor of Hyderabad; Charles Napier, the conqueror of Sind, 'a very advantageous useful, humane piece of rascality' as he described it himself in advance; David Baird of Seringapatam, and Colin Campbell, whose moderation ended the most brutal period of retribution after the Mutiny. Officers such as Colonel Pennington who completed 32 years of sevice could augment pay and prize money by private trade. He went home with a pension and £25,000 invested in the India Funds, but few lived long enough to enjoy their retirement. The 'English' graveyards are filled with memorials to the young men who died in India.

The nabobs of Scottish tradition were the merchants. Some, like John Farquahar, went out to Bombay as a cadet in the Company' s army in 1750 but switched to industry. Dealing in gunpowder, he left a fortune of £1,500,000. Legally, only East India Company agents who held 'writerships' could act as merchants. They worked for the Company but were allowed to trade privately. Agencies were secured by patronage and when Henry Dundas became President of the Board of Control in 1784 patronage was firmly in the hands of the Scots. He 'Scoticized India and Orientalized Scotland'. Sir John Macpherson became the first Governor General, to be followed by Lord Minto and the Marquis of Dalhousie. Governors of Madras and Bombay included Jonathan Duncan, Mountstuart Elphinstone, Sir Thomas Monro and Sir John Malcolm. Salaries were high and life magnificent.

Patronage secured a foot on the ladder for hundreds of impecunious young Scots and jobs higher up the scale for an older generation in financial trouble at home. The Grants of Rothiemurchus were typical. Elizabeth Grant in *The Memoirs of a Highland Lady* tells the story. Charles Grant became Chairman of the Directors of the East India Company in 1805. In 1828 Sir Peter, her father, had run up debts of £60,000 and was in exile in France when 'news came that he had been appointed to a judgeship in Bombay. Charles Grant, now Lord Glenelg, had done it.' Arriving in India, the family was greeted by rows of bowing servants sent by 'Uncle Edward' who had started his career as a cadet in the Company's army. 'Fortunately Charles Grant was able to change his appointment and gave him a writership.' A writership could be a licence for making money if the man survived the 'two monsoons' which were the traditional newcomer's lifespan in India. Fortunes could be restored and new ones made.

'If this be exile it is splendid exile,' wrote Elizabeth. It was also the best marriage market in the Empire where she and her sisters found suitors queuing up for them. She paints a clear picture of an upper-class society of merchants, administrators and soldiers, still largely male and integrating as far as they could with the highly cultured upper classes of India. They might have an Indian family and children whom they educated, but most were looking for a British bride to whom they could eventually go home.

Amongst the Scots were scholars and scientists of high distinction. Studying Sanskrit and Persian, they wrote some of the first histories of India and as archaeologists uncovered much that had been lost. Colin Campbell made the first geographical survey of India, Alexander Dalrymple became Hydrographer to both the East India Company and the Royal Navy, and Alexander Kydd

A 'Chummery' of the Bombay and Burma Trading Company in 1891. Bachelor employees of firms in India and Burma lived in these residences with their personal servants until the 1950s.

created the Botanic Gardens in Calcutta. They contributed to a culture which they respected.

When English replaced Persian as the language of the Company in the 1830s the political and social climate changed. Dalhousie reversed the Company's policy of non-interference in Indian customs. His westernizing reforms and the legacy of fear left by the Mutiny in 1857 erected barriers which never came down. Patronage was replaced by entry into the service by competitive exams and the East India Company's monopoly of trade was ended. But Scots continued to play a disproportionately important role in the government of India. Seven of the twelve viceroys were Scots and graduates went out as judges, district officers, and administrators to enforce English law, codified and adapted by Thomas Macaulay to Indian society. Engineers developed her roads, railways and canals, and academics her universities and schools. And the wives of the Scottish missionaries opened up the possibility of education for girls.

Burma was less important for the Scot in search of a job. Lower Burma was annexed in 1852, Upper Burma in 1886. Again it was a case of the flag following trade. Thomas Findlay and Son had established a trading station at Moulmein in 1839. In the 1840s, in partnership with James Buchanan, the son of a former Virginia tocacco merchant, they were shipping coal, textiles, salt and glass from the Clyde and bringing back teak and rice. The Burma Oil Company was registered in Edinburgh in 1886 and owned 95% of British Petroleum, forging links with Grangemouth and the oil industry. Amongst many engineers who came out from Scotland was Col Alexander Fraser who rebuilt Rangoon and, on the model of Skerryvore, built the lighthouse at the mouth of the Irrawady River which still marks the entrance to the Bay of Bengal. But Burma was never Scotticized.

Towards the end of the century some real settlers arrived in India – the tea and coffee planters of the south. Running estates for great Glasgow firms like Findlay's – sometimes acquiring

Colonel James Skinner with one of his sons holding a regimental Durbar at Hansi, painted by Gulam Ali Singh in 1827.

their own – they lived isolated lives up in the hills. Like all the British in India they sent their children home to be educated. Wives had to choose between abandoning their husbands or their families. But when India became independent in 1947 many stayed on; India had become their home. For most Scots it had been a love affair. Back in Britain they still yearn for the sun – and the servants. The heat and the dust and the heartbreak of broken homes have often been forgotten.

10 Africa

The Mediterranean shores of Africa were known to medieval scholars but it was the sixteenth century before its southern coastlines were becoming familiar to traders making the long sea journey to India. The hinterland was unknown territory, the Dark Continent. Sir John Henderson of Fordell ventured into it in the 1620s and 'was delivered into slavery by a barbarian in Zanquebar ... when a princess of that countrie falling in love with him even to renouncing her religion and countrie contrived the means of both their escapes'. The slave trade was a strong disincentive to exploration and in the early eighteenth century Jonathan Swift could write:

Geographers in Afric maps
With savage pictures fill their gaps
And o'er inhabited downs
Place elephants for want of towns.

By the end of the century Scots were replacing elephants with rivers and lakes and exploration was to be their major contribution to European rule in Africa.

The first of the Scottish explorers was attracted to Africa by his classical education. James Bruce of Kinnaird, while British consul in Tripoli in 1763, was commissioned by George I to record antiquities. In the 1770s this led him to Egypt and a search, dressed as an Arab doctor, for the source of the Nile. His descriptions of Abyssinia and the Blue Nile undermined the picture of 'the noble savage' and were widely disbelieved. But his *Travels* inspired Sir Joseph Banks to found 'The African Association' in 1788. It sponsored Mungo Park, an East India Company ship's surgeon from Selkirk, in his exploration of Gambia and Senegal. He too was captured by Arabs but, escaping with a horse and a compass, he reached the Niger. His *Travels in the Interior of Africa* stimulated government funding. He learnt Arabic and, in 1805, explored 1,000 miles of the Niger in a canoe. All but one of the 38 men who set out with him died. Richard Lander, who completed Park's work some years later, was also killed. In the 1870s Macgregor Laird, the son of a Glasgow shipowner, opened up the river to steam navigation and trade.

James Bruce , traveller and explorer in Africa, as depicted by John Kay.

By the nineteenth century the curiosity of the born explorer was being reinforced by Christian missions, the antislavery movement and the search for markets and raw materials for a rapidly industrializing Britain. Government money and ships of the Royal Navy were increasingly made available for exploration. In 1823 Captain Hugh Clapperton got as far as Lake Chad in his search for an overland route from the Western Sudan to Tripoli; in 1828 Major Gordon Lang reached Timbuktu; in 1864 James Grant was the first white man to cross equatorial Africa. But the most remarkable achievement was David Livingstone's. Trading in slaves became illegal in the Empire in 1807 and possession of slaves was banned in 1833. But the trade continued. Livingstone believed that only by bringing Christianity to the people of Africa could it be stopped. His *Missionary Travels and Researches in South*

Africa, published in 1857, fired the imagination of the public and put pressure on governments to assist exploration.

In 'one man's advance on the African continent' he traversed a third of its surface, recording with meticulous care everything he observed. He explored the main lakes and the river systems, crossed the Kalahari desert, opened up routes for missionaries to follow and published, after each great journey, a journal describing his discoveries in south, east and central Africa. Starting as a missionary, he recognized the need for financial backing and for the development of an African economy which would be an alternative to the lucrative slave trade. 'I go back to Africa to make a path for commerce and Christianity.'

As traders, Scots came late on the scene. Hugh Clapperton secured a commercial treaty with the Sultan of Western Sudan in the 1820s, Glasgow merchants set up the African Lakes Company 'to advance the word of God by honest trade' in the 1860s, and Macgregor Laird's United Africa Company was operating on the Niger in the 1890s. Scottish manufactured goods went out and tea, coffee, palm oil, cotton, sugar and rice came back. But the climate of tropical Africa ruled out the possibility of long-term settlement by the men who went out to run these companies.

In Cape Colony, purchased from the Dutch in 1814, the climate was excellent and the government encouraged emigration, hoping to create a barrier against black Africa. The first settlement of discharged Scots soldiers, who introduced merino sheep, rapidly intermarried and integrated with the Protestant Boers. In 1817 Benjamin Moodie brought out 200 Scots – some as indentured servants – to farm smallholdings at Albany on the frontier. Two more shiploads followed but, in spite of financial aid from the government, the attempt to establish a Scottish community failed. In 1849 a third attempt to create a settlement by two ministers and 127 people from the Maclean estates on Coll was equally unsuccesful. Land in South Africa was unsuitable for smallholdings and there was no market for cheap white labour: farming required capital on a scale which few would-be Scottish emigrants could supply. This was equally true of land in the eastern highlands of the growing Empire. Scots played a very small part as settlers in British possessions in Africa; the work of individuals as administrators, teachers, doctors and journalists was far more significant.

Of early governors, Sir George Gray in Cape Colony and Sir Claude Macdonald in Nigeria pursued forward policies and Sir Charles Eliott, in the East African Protectorate, played an important role in encouraging the development of the cash crops which paid for the building of the railway. Higher education was established in the Cape by 1821 and primary and technical schools in the mission stations by the mid-century. Thomas Pringle and John Fairburn

Jane Waterston, who grew up in Inverness in the 1840s and '50s, became a teacher and doctor in southern Africa

fought a successful battle against attempts to censor the Press and, by the twentieth century, Scots in their hundreds were serving as soldiers, foresters and administrators. There were the black sheep too and those Scots of whom it is difficult to be proud like Cecil Rhodes' close ally Dr Jameson. Having made a fortune in the gold and diamond mines of the Transvaal, he led a filibustering raid designed to overthrow the Boer government. It failed miserably. With Livingstone one is on surer ground. A writer in the *Anthropological Review* of 1866 described him as 'a poor, naked mind bedaubed with the chalk and red ochre of Scotch theology and with a threadbare tattered waistcoat of education hanging around him'. But his work has stood the test of time. On the centenary of his death in 1973 six African countries issued commemorative stamps.

11 The missionaries

Celtic monks restored Christianity to much of Western Europe in the seventh and eighth centuries but it was a thousand years before Scots returned to the mission field in significant numbers. Although James VI and I had ordered that 'The word of God and Service be preached, planted and used as well in the said colonies as also as much as might be among the savages bordering among them', missionary activity in America was minimal. Jesuits, Moravians, Dutch and Danes were active throughout the known world, but British missionary outreach only gathered impetus in the eighteenth century and was mainly Anglican.

Scottish involvement came in the nineteenth century. Exposure to Hindu and Muslim religions in India roused missionary fervour but it was checked by the East India Company's policy of non-interference in a sophisticated culture. In Africa the horrors of the slave trade challenged the conscience of the church, and the Africa Society was funding missionaries long before Britain owned territory on the continent. The Evangelical movement turned devout Christians to the mission field, their confidence fuelled by increasing wealth and successful empire building.

Missionary societies proliferated – Edinburgh and Glasgow in 1796, the Church of Scotland Society in 1829 and a dynamic Free Kirk Society after the Disruption of 1843. Their role was to plan missionary activity, to finance mission stations and to recruit and train the men, and increasingly the women, who left Scotland to teach, preach and serve in any part of the heathen world to which British power or trading connections gave them access. The Assembly of the Church of Scotland gave the movement its blessing in 1824 and increasingly wealthy middle-class congregations financed it. Inspiration came from men like Alexander Duff, the first professor of missions at New College, Edinburgh:

And would you keep your spiritual sympathies pent up within the craggy ramparts of the Grampians? ... Let us awake, arise and revive the genius of olden times: ... Like them let us enter into a

Solemn League and Covenant before our God on behalf of that benighted land that we will not rest till the voices of praise and thanksgiving arise in daily orisons from its coral strands, roll over its fertile plains, resound from the smiling villages and re-echo from its everlasting hills.

Duff had been working in India since 1830. The English Baptist William Carey's mission in the 1790s had been amongst the lower castes and he had translated the Bible into their languages. He initiated the policy of training converts for the ministry and tried to foster 'every kind of genius and grace in them'. Duff set out to convert the higher castes through education. The school he founded, Madras College, was to become the first missionary college in India. Study of the Bible was central, but great stress was placed on science and English literature. Its graduates were qualified for entry into British universities and employment in the Raj. Many of the ministers who followed Duff, fine Oriental scholars like John Wilson and Stephen Hislop, were critical of the denigration of Indian culture which was too often the result of the westernization of higher education which Duff had initiated.

From the start of the century the women who went out with their husbands played an important role in education and nursing care. Mrs Hislop and Mrs Wilson, the latter an early student of Aberdeen University, worked amongst women in purdah and started the first school for girls in Bombay. In Africa women such as Mrs Livingstone taught hygiene and elementary nursing skills to native tribes and taught in schools where blacks and whites were integrated. But the threat posed to the health of Europeans by the climate of tropical Africa was real. After a brief life together in some remote mission station many families were broken up. The women and their children often went back to Scotland and many missionaries died, far from home, amongst the people to whom they had devoted their lives.

By the end of the century women, as missionaries in their own right, outnumbered men. It was one of the few careers open to a girl of strong personality and religious conviction. Dr Jane Waterston was a pioneer. She was sent out by the Free Kirk in 1866 to start a boarding school for girls at Lovedale in the Eastern Cape but later decided that she could serve African women better as a doctor. No university in England or Scotland would accept a woman medical student in the 1860s so she trained in Dublin and Belgium and returned to Nyasaland as the first woman doctor in the mission field. Another remarkable woman was Mary Hepburn-Scott who served in India for 52 years. In 1905 at Kalimpong she ran a mission camp single-handed, building bamboo huts, teaching, nursing and burying the dead during outbreaks of cholera and smallpox. At Sikkim, with the approval of its ruler, she built a church and a school which, in 1995, has over 1,000 pupils. When officially retired she returned to start a school for the blind. The Indian government awarded her the Kaisar-i-Hind gold medal, the British the MBE and St Andrews University the first Honorary Doctorate of Divinity to be awarded to a woman.

Mary Hepburn-Scott was the daughter of Lord Polwarth; Mary Slessor, a Dundee mill girl, opened the way for hundreds from less privileged backgrounds. She worked on the Calabar coast of west Africa 'penetrating uncharted areas, fearlessly denouncing slavery and human sacrifice to pagan gods, and working for better conditions for women in tribal societies where they are of little account'.

Scottish churches also made a mission career possible for men from poor families. Robert Moffat, son of an East Lothian gardener, and his son-in-law David Livingstone, who started work in a cotton mill when he was ten and was thirty before he had graduated in medicine, are classic examples but there were many more. Robert Laws was typical. Born in 1851, the son af an Aberdeenshire carpenter, his training in Arts, Theology and Medicine was financed by the Free Kirk and his own savings from work in the Glasgow Mission's Fever Hospital. In Africa he

Title page of Robert Moffat's Missionary Labours and Scenes in Southern Africa. *Moffat was one of the pioneering missionaries in Africa, and father-in-law of David Livingstone.*

MISSIONARY
LABOURS AND SCENES

IN

SOUTHERN AFRICA;

BY

ROBERT MOFFAT,

TWENTY-THREE YEARS AN AGENT OF THE LONDON MISSIONARY SOCIETY IN THAT
CONTINENT.

FOURTH THOUSAND.

Preaching at Mosheu's Village.—(See page 596.)

With Engravings, by G. Baxter.

LONDON:
JOHN SNOW, PATERNOSTER-ROW.

1842.

taught manual skills and introduced new crops as well as working as a medical missionary. A few years later David Brown, a brick-layer from Falkirk, saved enough of the money earned building skyscrapers in New York to start studying for the mission field. He died in Tanganyika in 1946 amongst hospitals, churches and schools whose building he had supervised and in which he had worked as doctor, minister and teacher.

Brown had taught the natives to lay bricks as well as to pray. From the early years of the century the missionaries realized that, if the slave trade were to be ended, predatory tribes had to have alternative ways of earning money. Moffat took a plough as well as a Bible into Bechuanaland; cash crops – cotton, rice, cocoa, innumerable fruits and vegetables – were introduced around mission stations to make it possible 'to advance the Kingdom of God by honest trade'. A printing press was set up and water and electricity brought into mission stations such as Lovedale and Livingstonia. An important contribution was made to the eco-nomic development of Africa.

There were some missionaries who fitted Dan Crawford's description. Himself a missionary, he wrote in 1900:

> Many a little Protestant Pope in the lonely bush is forced by his self-imposed isolation to be prophet, priest and king, all rolled into one ... really a very big duck he, in his own private pond ... Quite seriously, he is forced to be a bit of a policeman, muddled up in matters not even remotely his sphere.

Others were like Dr Goodall who, writing about Chief Khama of Bechuanaland who had been converted to Christianity, recog-nized that 'protecting Africans was not simply a matter of the strong protecting the weak; it was also a question of according the freedom and opportunity rightfully due to those who had their own distinctive contribution to make to the common weal'.

By the time Scottish ministers reached Australia there were few Aborigines to convert. In New Zealand missionaries going out in 1814 were opposed to colonial settlement and were successful in protecting the Maoris from some of its worst features. A training college was set up in Aukland in 1843 and most of the Maoris were reported to have been converted by the mid-century.

In China and Japan early Christian communities had been persecuted and doors were firmly closed to western influence until forced open by the Opium Wars of the 1840s and '50s. Robert Morrison, the first Protestant missionary to China, went out in 1807 as translator for the East India Company merchants trading from Canton. A brilliant linguist, he wrote a Chinese grammar, a six-volume dictionary, and translated, with the help of another Scot, William

Eric Liddell when a boy in China, where his parents were missionaries. An Olympic gold medallist, he returned to China to continue his parents' work.

Milne, the Old and the New Testaments. The college he founded in Malacca in 1820 was intended for the study of Chinese and English literature as well as for the training of native evangelists to work on the mainland which was still closed to Europeans. The dispensary he established with Chinese staff was the forerunner of the medical missions through which western medicine reached China. In the 1890s, reaction to westernization led to the Boxer Rising in which hundreds of missionaries and their families and thousands of converts were murdered. Many of the Scottish missionaries who returned to the field in the twentieth century suffered a similar fate. Enthusiasm for missionary work reached a peak before the First World War. The break-up of the Empire destroyed confidence and Cecil Rhodes' belief that 'we are the first race of the world and the more of the world we inhabit the better it is for the human race' became officially unacceptable. The best of the missionaries had rejected the Rhodes approach from the start. Scottish missionaries, working in Asia, Africa and the West Indies are now part of an ecumenical movement to build an international Church.

12 Australia

French explorers sighted Australia in the early sixteenth century and Van Diemen claimed the continent for the Netherlands a hundred years later. But when in 1769 Captain Cook charted the eastern coast of what was called New Holland the only inhabitants were the Aborigines. The British government saw it as an ideal dumping ground for the dregs of society who could no longer be shipped off to America. New South Wales, the penal colony, was founded.

Scots were amongst the earliest settlers but they came out as guards rather than prisoners. Scotland had no lack of criminals but they were dealt with more economically at home. Only the most hardened offenders and a few political prisoners were transported and there were twenty English convicts for every Scot. But as officers, officials and governors they played a major role in turning a prison into a colony. Captain John Hunter, Captain John MacArthur and Sir Lachlan Macquarie, who succeded Captain Phillip as governors of New South Wales, were humane men, determined that rehabilitation should be possible for prisoners who had completed their sentences. Often ignoring orders from London, they tried to create a society in which civilized life would be possible. Coming out in 1810 in command of the Black Watch, Macquarie found a colony 'barely emerging from imbecility' and in the 1820s a reviewer for *Blackwood's Magazine* described its inhabitants as 'murderous, monsterous, debased, burglarious, brutified, larcenous and pick-pocketous'. But the Scottish governors laid foundations on which a self-governing community could be built.

They had also started to explore 2,975,000 square miles of unknown territory. After landing the first shipload of convicts at

Sydney Cove in 1788 Phillip and Hunter set out into the hinterland and discovered the Hawksmore River and the Blue Mountains. They were followed by a distinguished company of explorers, naval officers, botanists and surveyors who pushed back the known frontiers to create an accurate map of Australia. James Grant and then James Murray commanded the *Lady Nelson* which sailed through the Bass Strait and along the south coast of the continent. A few years later Robert Brown, who had studied medicine at Edinburgh University, joined Captain Flinders as naturalist on the *Investigator*. He collected 31,400 specimens, half of them unknown, and his *Preliminary Work on the Flora of New Holland* became the foundation of the study of the botany of the Antipodes.

Alan Cunningham, the son of a Renfrewshire gardener, combined botany with major exploration. He came out from Kew as King's Botanist and, with the Surveyor General, Sir Thomas Mitchell, made a 1,200 mile exploration of the Lachlan River. In 1823 he discovered what was to become Queensland, the Darling Downs 'of a rich black and dry soil clothed with abundance of grass ... constituting a range of sheep pastures convenient to water but beyond the reach of floods'. MacArthur had already introduced Merino sheep; the Downs provided the rich grazing

The merino sheep was first brought to South Africa by Col Robert Gordon, then to Australia by another Scot, John Macarthur.

on which Australia's main cash crop – wool – could be produced. In his own words he 'strove to advance for years botanic science here, blending augmentation of our knowledge of the plants of the country with that of its internal geography'. Mitchell was an artist as well as an intrepid explorer. He produced the first reliable map of New South Wales, pushed west towards the deserts and north into tropical Australia and left a wonderful collection of drawings of Aborigines and their territory.

The most remarkable achievement was John MacDouall Stuart's. He had trained at the Naval and Military Academy in Edinburgh but was considered too small and frail for an army career and found work in the Survey Department in Adelaide. A reward was offered to the first person to cross the continent from south to north. In 1863, on his third attempt, he reached the site of Port Darwin and added another half million square miles to the Northern Territory. The editor of the *South Australian Advertiser* wrote:

> The interior of Australia was unknown. Was it a region of burning mountains, a desert of shifting sands ... Was it a sea or a lake or a fruitful country? Stuart said he would go and see and he returned to tell us.

He nearly died from scurvy on the return journey, but John MacKinlay, who explored Central Australia, suffered less. He used camels, introduced by Sir Thomas Elder the great wool merchant, to cross the desert. But most of the explorers died young, either in the course of their exploration or exhausted by its rigours. They had opened up the continent; the problem was how to people it.

In the 1820s the Australia Company of Leith was the main recruiting agent. The fortunes of the port had been badly damaged by competition from Glasgow, depression in the corn trade with the Baltic and the termination of the Forth and Clyde

Poster dated 1889 offering free and assisted passages. Assisted emigration was being offered by all the colonies by the end of the nineteenth century.

EMIGRANTS' INFORMATION OFFICE, 31, BROADWAY, WESTMINSTER, S.W.

POSTER.

1st October, 1888.

Office Open—

Every week day but Saturday 10.30 a.m. to 6.30 p.m.
Saturday 10.30 a.m. to 2 p.m. only.

NOTE.—This office has been established under the supervision of the Colonial Office for the purpose of supplying intending emigrants with useful and trustworthy information respecting emigration to the British Colonies. The information issued to the public is mainly obtained from the various Colonial Governments and their representatives in this country. No pains are spared to make the information as accurate as possible, but the committee of management cannot undertake to hold themselves responsible for the absolute correctness of every detail.

GENERAL INFORMATION
FOR INTENDING
EMIGRANTS
TO
CANADA, THE AUSTRALASIAN AND SOUTH AFRICAN COLONIES.

LENGTH AND COST OF PASSAGE.

The Time ordinarily taken on the voyage, and the lowest rate of unassisted passages to the above Colonies, are as follows:—

	BY STEAMER.		BY SAILING VESSEL.	
	Average Time.	Lowest Fare. (Liable to change) £ s. d.	Average Time.	Lowest Fare. (Liable to change) £ s. d.
CANADA	9-10 days	4 0 0		
NEW SOUTH WALES ...	45-52 ,,	14 14 0	About 3 months	13 13 0
VICTORIA	42-49 ,,	14 14 0	Nearly 3 months	13 13 0
SOUTH AUSTRALIA ...	40-46 ,,	14 14 0	,, 3 months	12 12 0
QUEENSLAND	45 ,,	15 15 0	About 3 months	15 3 0
WESTERN AUSTRALIA ..	35-40 ,,	16 16 0	,, 3 months	14 14 0
TASMANIA	40-50 ,,	14 14 0	,, 3 months	14 12 0
NEW ZEALAND	45 ,,	16 16 0	,, 3 months	13 13 0
CAPE	29 ,,	15 15 0		
NATAL	26-28 ,,	18 18 0		

PASSAGES.

1. FREE PASSAGES. — QUEENSLAND. — To selected unmarried Agricultural Labourers and single Female Domestic Servants (apply to the Agent General). No Free Passages to any other Colony.

2. ASSISTED PASSAGES. — WESTERN AUSTRALIA. — £10 is allowed to Farmers, Agriculturists, and others likely to be useful in country districts; but a deposit of not less than £100 (to be refunded on arrival in the Colony) is as a rule required before any assistance is given.

QUEENSLAND.—Assisted passages are given to unmarried labourers connected with the land, as Ploughmen, Gardeners, &c., and to Female Servants, at the following rates:—*Males*, 12 to 40, £8; 40 to 55, £12. *Females*, 12 to 40, £4; and 40 to 55, £12.

No assisted passages are given at the present time to CANADA, NEW SOUTH WALES, VICTORIA, SOUTH AUSTRALIA, TASMANIA, NEW ZEALAND, The CAPE or NATAL; but in the case of QUEENSLAND and the CAPE passages at lower rates are given, under special conditions, to Labourers engaged here by employers in these Colonies.

In the case of QUEENSLAND, Land Order Warrants to the value of £20 are given under certain conditions to persons paying their own passage direct to the Colony.

3. NOMINATED PASSAGES.—QUEENSLAND, WESTERN AUSTRALIA, and NATAL.—Residents in these Colonies can, under certain specified conditions, nominate their friends for Free Passages on making payments in the Colony as under:—

QUEENSLAND.—Males, 1 to 12 years of age, £2; 12 to 40, £4; 40 to 55, £8; Females, 1 to 12, £1; 12 to 40, £2; 40 to 55, £8. Confined to Agricultural and other Labourers connected with the land, and Female Domestic Servants.

WESTERN AUSTRALIA.—On payment of £7 to a limited number of Nominees, approved by the Crown Agents for the Colonies.

NATAL.—£12 per adult.

No Nominated Passages are at present given to CANADA, NEW SOUTH WALES, VICTORIA, SOUTH AUSTRALIA, TASMANIA, NEW ZEALAND, or The CAPE.

ARRANGEMENTS ON LANDING.

CANADA.—Depôts for emigrants are provided at the ports of Quebec and Halifax and the other principal towns in the Dominion.

NEW SOUTH WALES.—Apply to Mr. G. F. Wise, Immigration Agent, Hyde Park, Sydney.

QUEENSLAND.—There are Depôts at the principal ports and in various parts of the Colony, in which Government assisted emigrants are received free of charge for a few days after arrival.

WESTERN AUSTRALIA.—There is a Labour Registry Office at Perth where Emigrants should apply, but no Government Depôt for the reception of Emigrants is now open.

NEW ZEALAND.—There are Depôts at most of the principal ports for the reception of emigrants.

There are no Government Depôts in VICTORIA, SOUTH AUSTRALIA, TASMANIA, THE CAPE, or NATAL; but there are private agencies in some of these and the other Colonies, particulars of which are given in the Circulars.

BEST TIME FOR ARRIVING.

CANADA.—April to middle of July—not the Winter months.

NEW SOUTH WALES.—Any month—September to November for preference.

VICTORIA.—Ditto.

SOUTH AUSTRALIA.—May to October.

QUEENSLAND.—April to October inclusive.

WESTERN AUSTRALIA.—September to November. Any month—September to November for preference.

NEW ZEALAND.—September to January inclusive.

CAPE.—Any month—August for preference.

NATAL.—Any month—August for preference.

PRESENT DEMAND FOR LABOUR.

FARMERS WITH CAPITAL.—A demand in all the Colonies.

FARM LABOURERS.—A demand for good men in CANADA, NEW SOUTH WALES, VICTORIA, QUEENSLAND, TASMANIA, and some parts of NEW ZEALAND.

MECHANICS AND GENERAL LABOURERS.—Some demand in MELBOURNE, especially for men connected with the building trades. Little or no demand in any other Colony.

FEMALE DOMESTIC SERVANTS.—A good demand in most districts of Canada and the Australasian Colonies, and a slight one at The Cape. Particulars as to the state of the Labour Market in the various Colonies from time to time will be given in subsequent editions of this Poster.

NAMES AND ADDRESSES OF COLONIAL REPRESENTATIVES IN ENGLAND.

CANADA.—High Commissioner, 9, Victoria Chambers, Victoria Street, Westminster, S.W.

NEW SOUTH WALES.—Agent General, 5, Westminster Chambers, Victoria Street, S.W.

VICTORIA.—Agent General, 8, Victoria Chambers, Victoria Street, S.W.

SOUTH AUSTRALIA.—Agent General, 8, Victoria Chambers, Victoria Street, S.W.

QUEENSLAND.—Agent General, 1, Westminster Chambers, Victoria Street, S.W.

WESTERN AUSTRALIA.—The Crown Agents for the Colonies, Downing Street, S.W.

NEW ZEALAND.—Agent General, 7, Westminster Chambers, Victoria Street, S.W.

TASMANIA.—Agent General, 5, Westminster Chambers, Victoria Street, S.W.

CAPE.—Agent General, 7, Albert Mansions, Victoria Street, S.W.

NATAL.—Emigration Agent for Natal, 21, Finsbury Circus, E.C.

Further information can be obtained by writing or personally applying to the Chief Clerk at this office, 31, Broadway, Westminster, S.W., from whom the CIRCULARS issued by the Committee of Management respecting the separate Colonies can be obtained gratis, and the new HANDBOOKS, with Maps and fuller information, at the price of 1d. post free for each Colony.

Printed for Her Majesty's Stationery Office by W. P. GRIFFITH & SONS, LD., Prujean Square, Old Bailey, London, E.C.

Canal at Grangemouth. Plans were made to restore prosperity by triangular trade between the West Indies, New South Wales and Leith. This would provide a regular passenger service to the new colony and a market for Scottish manufactures. But, with fares at £75 cabin class and £30 steerage, it could only attract emigrants with considerable capital. £500 was the minimum possible and John Campbell, a magistrate of Perth who took out £8,000, was probably typical. He left Scotland with eight sons, five daughters, five men and fifteen women servants, shepherds, gardeners, smiths, ploughmen and cabinetmakers.

Later on a few skilled craftsmen were given free passages, but there could be no migration of whole communities until near famine conditions in the Highlands in the mid-century put pressure on the government to finance emigration. Then thousands of impoverished weavers from Clydeside and Perthshire and crofters from the north did go out to settle in Victoria and Queensland. The discovery of gold in the 1850s brought thousands more – so many Scots that every gully was reputed to have its piper – and a Gaelic paper circulated briefly in 1857. But within a generation the Highlanders were absorbed into a community whose Scottishness was to be kept alive by Caledonian societies rather than Gaelic.

Although the proportion of Scots in the population had dropped to about 15% by the end of the century, a visitor could still comment in 1892 on the influence of Scots. 'These people, the best of all British colonists, are found in all parts of the country and in many towns ... they control affairs and give the prevalent tone to society.' The Presbyterian church had made a vital contribution to this. John Dunmore Lang, joining his brother in Australia in 1823, wrote in his journal 'The climate is delightful, the country is highly productive, but its people – O generation of vipers! Will they never be warned to flee from the wrath to come?' Lang set out to warn them. As the first minister of the Presbyterian Church in Sydney he devoted his life to bringing out graduate ministers, setting up schools and persuading sober hard-working Scots to emigrate. 'It is hoped that every district will, in the course of time, be supplied with Schools to train up an educated, industrious, and orderly community.' Henry Carmichael, a graduate of St Andrews, made sure that the education should not be bigoted. 'My constant aim is to facilitate to the best of my power the process enabling each mind to form on all subjects (and on the subject of religion among the rest) opinions for itself.'

Men and women of this calibre created the infrastructure of a civilized society. Academies, for girls as well as boys, technical schools, and university chairs were founded and funded. In 1826 the first bookshop and the first lending library were opened by William MacGarvie while his brother John set up the dispensary which was to become Sydney Infirmary. The great Mitchell Library was founded at the beginning of the twentieth century with the 61,000 books left to the state of New South Wales by David Scott Mitchell, the son of a Fife doctor. Successful Scots were leading philanthropists.

In the economic development of the continent the pattern was similar. When Anthony Trollope visited his son in 1873 he wrote, 'Those who make money are generally Scotchmen.' Of these Robert Campbell of Greenock was the first and perhaps the most influential. Representing the family firm Campbell, Clark and Company, merchants in Calcutta, he leased land in Sydney Cove and imported cattle and horses from India. Dealing in whale and seal-oil and skins – the colony's first exports – he broke the East India Company's monopoly of trade with Australia and in 1815 Sydney became a free port. He was one of the founders of the Bank of New South Wales and Secretary of the Savings Bank for 'the Industrious Poor'. As early as 1804, 200 of his fellow settlers wrote 'But for you, we had still been a prey to the Mercenary, unsparing Hand of Avarice and Extortion.'

At the other end of the scale were the squatters who occupied land illegally. Buying sheep, often on borrowed capital, they drove their flocks into the outback until they found pasture unclaimed by other settlers. It was a life of appalling hardship only mitigated if they could find a wife to share the work. Catherine Dickson wrote home to her friends in Scotland, 'Tell them they will all get married if they come out here. Crippled ones, deaf and dumb, all get married over here.' Of the surviving settlers some made fortunes and many more were able, to quote Lang, 'to live in comfort and independence abroad instead of struggling with increasing poverty and privations at home'.

Behind the development of the economy were Scottish financiers who provided three-quarters of the capital invested in the colony in the nineteenth century. Shipping, engineering, mining, brewing, refrigeration were all dominated by men whose names have survived; the forgotten Scots were the failures and the black sheep. Alexander Kedslie could write to his grandson in 1864 'Your cousin has ended as we had feared – a drunken railway porter in Australia.' He disappeared from the family chronicles; it is the achievers we remember.

13 New Zealand

During his first great exploration of the South Pacific in 1768, Captain Cook sighted New Zealand before he reached Australia. But the Maoris, who had preceded him by nearly a thousand years, were warlike and highly organized: no place for a penal colony there. A small station for victualling and repairing ships grew up at the Bay of Islands in the north, but New Zealand was not formally annexed to Britain till 1840. The missionaries who came out in 1814 did all they could to stop colonization, knowing the damage it could do to native tribes. Writing in 1839 Dunmore Lang, the Presbyterian minister in Melbourne, described an unofficial settlement in North Island. 'With a few honourable exceptions it consists of the veriest refuse of the civilized world ... of runaway sailors, of runaway convicts, of convicts who have served their terms of bondage in one or other of the penal colonies, of fraudulent debtors who have escaped from their creditors in Sydney or Hobart Towns and of needy adventurers from the two colonies, equally unprincipled.'

After 1840 government policies changed. Gibbon Wakefield's New Zealand Association, founded in 1838, had been buying land from the Maoris, selling it to farmers and using the money raised to assist the migration of the skilled craftsmen needed to build up a stable community. Fearing a French take-over of the Islands, Britain reached a compromise with the Maoris. Their land rights were guaranteed in exchange for recognition of British sovereignty. Under a series of Scottish governors this opened the way for exploration and settlement and, perhaps inevitably, to increasing conflict with the Maoris. Their concept of ownership was communal, which made sales of land by individuals invalid. By the time the wars ended in 1872 the Maori population had dropped from between 100,000 and 200,000 at the beginning of the century to 37,000. Sir David MacLean, as Minister for Native Affairs, had been responsible for the excessive purchases of land which had caused the wars but his Land Acts stabilized the situation, giving security to both settlers and Maoris. In 1867 they were given representation in the Legislature and, in theory at least, became equal citizens.

Scottish settlement was becoming significant by the mid-century. The Paisley Company had bought land and sent out three shiploads of emigrants in 1839; in the 1850s the government disarmed the Free Kirk's opposition to colonization by asking it to cooperate in the creation of a community at Otago Bay in South Island. This became Dunedin and attracted Scots from other parts of New Zealand. Captain Cargill, acting for the Lay Association of the Free Kirk, bought up 2,400 plots of 60 acres each and John Adam, their agent in Scotland, recruited 2,000 settlers from Mull and the west to farm the land. Of the money raised by sales, 12% went to the building and staffing of schools and churches.

Within a few years Dunedin had its own Medical School, but doctors practising in the early years had usually worked their way

*Rattray Street, Dunedin, in 1862, with hints of Edinburgh's
Georgian New Town in some of the buildings.*

out on emigrant boats. On one sailing from the Clyde the surgeon
was paid £25, but forfeited £1 for every passenger who died on
the voyage. Until steam replaced sail towards the end of the
century the journey out must have been a very frightening experience, but legislation was making conditions on emigrant ships
less appalling than they had been earlier. One doctor who came
out in 1842 made his name in politics rather than medicine. Sir
David Monro farmed 14,000 sheep on the 13,000 acres of land he
bought for £1,200. After seven years he wrote 'I have never entertained the idea of making this country my permanent home –
God forbid, I loathe the place.' But he stayed on to become a
member of the House of Representatives and was knighted for his
services as its Speaker.

Monro came from a landowning family in Easter Ross; John
Barr, an early settler in Otago, looked at New Zealand from a less
sophisticated background:

When to New Zealand first I cam
    Puir and duddy, puir and duddy
When to New Zealand first I cam
    It wis a happy day sirs.
For I wis fed on parritch thin
    Ma taes they stickit thro' ma shoon
I riggit at the pouken pin
But I couldna mak it pay, sirs.

Nae mair the laird comes far his rent
    Far his rent, far his rent,
Nae mair the laird comes far his rent
    When I hae nocht tae pay, sirs
Nae mair he'll tak me aff the loom
    Wi'hanging lip and pouches toom
Tae touch ma hat and boo tae him
The like wis never kent, sirs.

At my door cheek there's bread and cheese
    I work or no just as I please
I'm fairly settled at my ease
    And that's the way o't noo, sirs.

By the end of the century a prosperous economy had been built up on timber, sheep and refrigerated dairy products. Emigrants like John Barr helped to create a democratic society in which, by 1893, the franchise was extended to women as well as men. Legislation was passed to exclude absentee landowners, and old-age pensions, national insurance, medical services and industrial arbitration were introduced in New Zealand before they were in Britain.

Behind the liberalizing reforms which led to dominion status in 1907 was a series of Scottish politicians and public servants. One of these was Sir James Hector, Director of the Geological Survey and first Chancellor of the University of New Zealand. With his assistants John McKerrow, Quintin Mackinnon and Donald Sutherland, he explored and mapped much of New

James Macandrew, who emigrated to New Zealand in 1850, and helped to found the country's first university.

Zealand. Less reputable was James Mackenzie who explored the Snowy Mountains and Canterbury Plains. A Rossshire Gaelic speaker and a brother of the Sheriff of Melbourne, he reached New Zealand with enough money to buy land but not to stock it. He solved this problem by stealing 1,500 to 2,000 sheep and driving them, with the help of one dog and a bullock, into previously unmapped territory through what became known as Mackenzie's Gap. Thrice captured and thrice escaping – encumbered by fifteen-pound leg irons – he was eventually brought to trial. Claiming a right to silence, he refused to speak in court. The sentence passed on him was cancelled and he returned to Australia – another black sheep. In 1901 there were 48,000 people of Scottish origin in New Zealand, 43,000 from Ireland and 111,000 from England and Wales.

In the twentieth century New Zealand continued to attract a disproportionate number of Scots. Unemployment and limited opportunities drove them out, assisted passages made emigration possible along with societies such as the one founded by Norman McLeod in 1871. Its object had been 'To keep up the customs, traditions and language of the mother country, Highland dancing, games etc and to assist any immigrants from the Highlands of Scotland or Nova Scotia who settle in Waipu and are in need of help.' In a small country of mountains and sea, with a Presbyterian and democratic flavour, Scots could feel at home.

The Settler's Guide to New Zealand, *with scenes of peaceful rural life to tempt the emigrant.*

14 The rest of the world

Where else have Scottish emigrants gone? The first great movement was to Ireland, when James VI and I encouraged erstwhile reivers and sober Lowland farmers to leave and settle in Ulster. In the 1640s Wentworth, the English Governor, believed that there were 50,000 of them but the number was probably nearer 20,000. By the mid-eighteenth century many of them had crossed the Atlantic to become the Scotch Irish in America. Less dramatic but numerically more significant was the steady movement of Scots to England. In Ireland, language and religion prevented assimilation into the Catholic community and political and social power was restricted to Episcopalians; in England they rapidly became English. Going south is still the easiest move for Scots of all social classes to make.

Perhaps the most difficult move has always been to countries outside Britain's direct sphere of influence. The large number of Scots who served in the Merchant Navy or were involved in foreign trade became aware of opportunities throughout the world. Risks were high, but Scottish finance and financiers,

entrepreneurs and engineers could be found in Asia, South America and the Far East. The Glovers of Fraserburgh were typical. In 1857 Thomas Blake Glover went out to Japan as an agent for the Glasgow firm of shippers, Jardine Matheson. Educated in the Grammar School of Old Aberdeen, where engineering was taught as well as classics, he came from a sea-going family. His father was a senior coastguard and two

John Muir left Dunbar as a boy. An early conservationist, his work in the USA led to the creation of National Parks in the early twentieth century.

Glovers, probably uncles, were already in the East, one captaining a Matheson boat operating from Foochow and the other a customs officer at Canton. His brothers trained as shipwrights and followed him out to Japan. By 1861 Thomas had his own company, trading in seaweed, silk, coal, ships, ammunition and gold. He became an important link in the transfer of technology from industrialized Scotland to a Japan which was emerging rapidly from feudalism. As advisor to the Mitsubishu engineering firm and honoured by the Emperor, he died in Tokyo in 1911. With a Japanese son, to whose mother he was not legally married, he would have found it difficult to return to Presbyterian Fraserburgh. But most Scots working outside the Empire kept up their links with Scotland and planned to come home for retirement.

This was also true of South America. It had been virtually closed to British adventurers until the break-up of the Spanish and Portuguese Empires in the early nineteenth century. A

Dr Neil Gordon Munro graduated in Edinburgh but spent most of his life in Japan. Here he is treating an Ainu elder at his home in Nibutani Hokkaido. Fosco Maraini, 1940

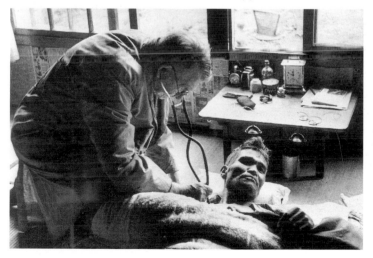

number of Scots did all they could to assist the break-up. In political trouble at home, Lord Thomas Cochrane went out to Chile in 1817 and offered his skills as a naval commander to the Chilean rebels. He destroyed 28 Spanish ships off the coast of Peru and returned to a hero's welcome in Valparaiso. A few years later he was fighting with the Brazilians in their struggle for independence from the Portuguese. In Venezuela Sir Gregor MacGregor was presented by Bolivar with the Medal of the Order of Libertadores in recognition of his services. He had persuaded Indian tribes to support the rebels and had led them into battle, pipes playing and kilts swinging.

Less successful was his attempt to settle 200 Scots in territory north of Panama in 1823. As ill planned as the Darien scheme, it was a similar disaster but on a smaller scale. A year later two brothers from Kelso, John and William Parish Robertson, nearly succeeded at Monte Grande, a few kilometres from Buenos Aires. The *Symmetry* sailed from Leith with a party of carefully chosen and well-equipped emigrants and a contract from the Argentinian government. For three years the settlers flourished, introducing advanced farming and fruit-growing methods to their farms by the River Plate. Failure to develop the economy of the emerging South American republic was due, as was so often the case, to its political instability and limited internal markets. The freedom of worship the settlers had been promised was granted but not the financial help. Having traded successfully in Chile, Peru, Argentina, Paraquay and Uruquay Robertson returned to Glasgow in 1830 with no more than 'the two guineas in his pocket' with which he had left Greenock in 1807. It was the second part of the century before fortunes were made, but the Scots who remained introduced methods of drainage and cross-breeding which were to transform Argentinian agriculture. Their experiments in processing and refrigeration opened up the European market to South American meat.

Trading contacts had been developing since the Napoleonic Wars when a third of British exports had been diverted to American markets. Opportunities for engineers to build railways, bridges and docks opened up as the republics developed. The first steam ship to sail on Lake Titicaca – 1,600 metres above sea level and separated from the coast by the range of the Andes – was 'reassembled there by Indians under the direction of a dour Scottish engineer who knew neither Spanish nor Aymara'. He was one of many for whom language, climate, culture and religion made assimilation difficult. With money in his pocket he would return to Scotland.

Emigrants to the USA rarely did. Between 1815 and 1914 thirteen million Scots are believed to have gone to the States, four million to Canada and one and a half million to Australia. Why? The fare to the Antipodes and the length of the journey were daunting but why to the States rather than Canada? There were no assisted passages and few Scottish communities waiting to welcome newcomers. But opportunities for skilled men were greater in an already partially settled country, especially in its booming cities. Wages were higher and the climate less harsh. For the un-enfranchised working man, leaving a country still dominated by a privileged landowning class, the States, rather than Canada, may have seemed the land of freedom. When steam power made the crossing shorter and cheaper, more came back, but those who settled made a disproportionate contribution to its political and economic development. Though St Andrew's Societies flourished, the Scot rapidly became an American.

As late as 1913 50% of those who emigrated to the USA were skilled workers, 21% were professionals and only 29% labourers. Increasingly, throughout the world, doors have been closed against the poor and unskilled, and Commonwealth countries no longer welcome whole communities moving from the Highlands. The last emigrant boat has sailed, but the brain drain continues. Scotland is still producing more highly qualified young people than her economy can absorb and the remnants of the Empire can no longer employ them. The majority look for work in England, but thousands are scattered across the globe as doctors, engineers and teachers of English. Thousands more pursue research, for which funding or facilities have been difficult to find in Britain, in universities abroad. Scotland lost over two million people in the twentieth century and too many of them were the most highly qualified.

But perhaps the wheel has come full circle. In the Middle Ages the able and ambitious Scot looked to mainland Europe for an escape from poverty. There are no barriers to the enterprising in the European Union and the Scot may again look for opportunities there. Or might communication technology transform an economy so long impoverished by its geography? Scotland, in the twenty-first century, could become a country in which the most gifted people stay at home.

FURTHER READING

BERG, J and LAGENCRANTZ BO *Scots in Sweden*, Edinburgh 1962

BROCK, W *Scotus Americanus*, Edinburgh 1982

BUMSTEAD, JM *The People's Clearance*, Edinburgh 1982

BURTON, JH *The Scot Abroad*, Edinburgh 1864

CAGE, RA (ed) *Scots Abroad, Labour, Capital and Enterprise*, London 1985

CAIN, AM *The Corn Chest for Scotland*, Edinburgh 1986

CALDER, J *The Scottish Soldier. Bonny Fighters*, Edinburgh 1987

CASSAVATI, E *The Lions and the Lilies*, London 1987

CUNNINGHAM, IC *Scotland and Africa*, Edinburgh 1982

DEVINE, T (ed) *Scottish Emigration and Scottish Society, The Emigrant Scot*, Edinburgh 1992

DONALDSON, G *The Scots Overseas*, London 1966

FISCHER, TA *Scots in Germany*, Edinburgh 1902

HEWAT, E *Vision and Enterprise*, Edinburgh 1960

HILL, D *Great Emigrations*, London 1972

HOOK, A *Scotland and America*, Glasgow 1975

MACKAY, A *Scottish Samurai*, Edinburgh 1993

MACMILLAN, D *Scotland and Australia*, Oxford 1967

MACMILLAN, D *Land of Exiles: Scots in Australia*, Edinburgh 1988

MACRAE, A *The Scots in Burma*, Edinburgh 1990

Michael, F *Les Ecossais en France, les Français en Ecosse*, 2 vols 1862

ROBERTS, EED (ed) *The Caledonian Phalanx*, Edinburgh 1987

SMAILES, H *The Scottish Empire*, Edinburgh 1981

STEUART, AF *Scots in Poland*, Edinburgh 1915

WILKIE, J *Metagama*, Edinburgh 1987

WOOD, S *The Scottish Soldier*, Manchester 1987

PLACES TO VISIT

Aberdeen: *Gordon Highlanders Regimental Museum*

Ardesier, Inverness-shire: *Queen's Own Highlanders Regimental Museum*

Banchory, Aberdeenshire: *Crathes Castle*. Contains painted ceilings, direct result of Baltic trade.

Bishopbriggs, Glasgow: *Thomas Muir Museum*. Muir, a radical lawyer, was transported to Botany Bay.

Blantyre, Glasgow: *David Livingstone Centre*

Broughton, Lanarkshire: *John Buchan Centre*. John Buchan was Governor General of Canada.

Culross, Fife: a harbour-town that grew up as trade expanded in the 16th century.

Dunfermline, Fife: *Andrew Carnegie Birthplace*

Dysart, Fife: *McDouall Stuart Museum*

Edinburgh: *Scottish National Portrait Gallery*

Edinburgh: *Royal Scots Museum, Edinburgh Castle*

Edinburgh: *Royal Museum of Scotland.* Contains material brought or sent back by Scots abroad

Edinburgh: *Scottish United Services Museum*, Edinburgh Castle

Edinburgh: *Scottish Record Office*

Glasgow: *Royal Highland Fusiliers Regimental Museum*

Andrew Carnegie left Dunfermline in 1848. Out of the fortune he made in the steel industry he funded scholarships and libraries in Scotland.

Greenock, Renfrewshire: *McLean Museum and Art Gallery*

Huntly, Aberdeenshire: *Craigievar Castle*. Built by a successful Aberdeen merchant.

Menstrie, Clackmannanshire: *Menstrie Castle*. Contains material on the Nova Scotia baronetcies.

Newburgh, Fife: *Laing Museum*. Contains material on emigration.

Newtonmore, Inverness-shire: *Clan Macpherson House and Museum*

Perth: *Black Watch Museum*

Sleat, Skye: *Clan Donald Centre* Stirling: *Argyll and Sutherland Highlanders Regimental Museum*, Stirling Castle

Stromness, Orkney: *Stromness Museum*

Symbister, Shetland: *The Pier House*. Contains material on Hanseatic trade.

In addition to material related to Scots abroad currently on display at the NMS Royal Museum of Scotland and Scottish United Services Museum, the new Museum of Scotland, due to open in late 1998, will feature several displays linked to the theme of Leaving Scotland.